SUSPECT ZERO

by

Michael D. Kelleher

First Edition (2003)

DEDICATION

For his many victims, so young and precious.

Introduction

In 1968, a serial killer with the moniker "Zodiac" began his career with a double homicide in the city of Vallejo, California, just east of San Francisco. Within a year, he had attacked seven people, mostly young couples, killing five. In a series of bizarre and disturbing letters to the San Francisco *Chronicle,* he would eventually lay claim to more than three-dozen victims. In 1978, after two-dozen letters, Zodiac disappeared, leaving investigators confused and empty-handed.

While an army of law enforcement personnel was busy chasing Zodiac, another series of murders was taking place less than an hour north of San Francisco, in the semi-rural community of Santa Rosa. Between early 1972 and late 1973, at least seven girls and young women were slain in a similar way by an unknown male assailant. Because Zodiac had attacked at a variety of locations around the Bay Area, including Vallejo, Lake Berryessa, and San Francisco, many investigators assumed that the Santa Rosa murders were also his doing (although the fugitive himself never took credit for them). These crimes came to be known in the press as the Highway 101 Murders. As with the Zodiac killings, the case has never been officially closed.

But even unsolved cases sometimes find a resolution. For there is a sea of certainty and understanding that lives forgotten or ignored between what is known and what can be proved. This was definitely true with the Highway 101 Murders.

And when traditional justice fails due to unexpected circumstances, lack of hard facts, insufficient resources, or unremitting confusion, there is still the possibility of discovered truth. What happened a few years ago in Sonoma County, California, is cause enough to believe in that possibility, even when fiction must, of necessity, take the reins from fact.

Death is Not a Christmas Present

Manny Bruin pushed his battered, squeaky chair away from the undersized desk until its back bumped against the wall behind him. Impelled by the force of his 215-pound bulk, the chair's gray metal frame dug into the plaster, deepening the long gouge that had formed from years of abuse. He tilted his thick head back, resting it against the wall, and slid the palm of his right hand across his forehead. It was warm and damp to the touch. The lieutenant wasn't feeling very well. In fact, he hadn't felt well all week.

Bruin let out a sigh and glanced down at his crotch. It was half-hidden by a middle age paunch that he couldn't seem to control anymore. Unwillingly, he let his eyes creep closed and rested his stubby hands in his lap, left over right. In the darkness behind his eyelids, Bruin had only a single thought to carry him away. It was December 18, 1980 — a week before Christmas. As usual, he had nothing to show for it. No shopping, no ideas, no gifts, nothing but a vague belief that some idiot had invented this holiday for his personal torment.

The lieutenant shuffled his head from side to side, rubbing against the wall behind him. Long ago, the wall had been a pristine white, but now it was gray and rough. Frustrated, he sighed loudly and shuffled around in the undernourished, noisy chair, trying to get comfortable. He had to get his mind off this thing. He needed something else to think about — anything but Avion, and Christmas.

"Lieutenant..." She hummed at him from the doorway, offering him a deep, rhythmic sound that was both familiar and unwelcome. Bruin closed his eyes tighter. Maybe she'd just go away.

"Lieutenant," she repeated, an octave higher. He could hear her shuffling her big, flat feet back and forth across the paper-thin carpeting. The nightstick on her belt rattled against the doorframe. Bruin pushed his head forward and reluctantly opened his eyes, pulling his chair back toward the desk with a burly left hand.

"Yeah, Sherry... sorry... I've got a few things on my mind." He didn't bother looking at her.

She hummed again, this time with a hint of understanding. She slipped into the tiny office, positioned herself directly in front of his desk and forced him to look at her. His expression was nondescript and uncomfortable; his eyes were drawn and dark.

"Sergeant Millian is on line four, sir. He didn't want to leave a message. He says he needs to talk to you *now*."

The lieutenant rolled his head to the left and stared at the ebony phone perched on the edge of the desk. Line 4 was blinking at him furiously.

"Okay, good, thanks..." he said flatly, nodding a dismissal toward the open office door. She spun around and slipped away to her desk, just outside his office. Bruin reached for the phone.

"Hi Mick," said Manny. "What's going on?" This was his best lieutenant's voice, carefully constructed to sound sure and ready.

"Hey, Manny," said Millian. "Listen, I've got a good one for you. This will make your day..." He paused, tempting Bruin with silence.

"Yeah, well, if you say so," Bruin answered hoarsely. "Just about *anything* would make my day right now."

"Well," Millian began, "I'm standing about two feet from a corpse, Manny, and I think you'll..."

"What?!" Bruin shouted. "I didn't hear about any homicide!"

"Whoa... slow down... take it easy," said Millian. "It's not a *homicide*, Manny, it's a natural. Or at least it looks that way to me. What you want to know is *who* he is."

"Okay, okay... sorry, Mick. So, who is it? And, *please*, none of your Santa Claus jokes. I'm not in the mood."

"It's Byron Avion."

The phone rattled around in Bruin's fingers, nearly falling to the desktop. He steadied his hand and moved the phone back to his mouth.

"Are you kidding me, Mick? Is this a joke?"

"Nope. It's Avion. I'm looking at his dead body right now."

More silence. Bruin's mind raced. Suspect Zero. A thousand pictures flashed by. The names of the dead — the places their bodies were discovered. Avion's tight, unsteady smile. That room in the basement.

"You're sure this wasn't a homicide, Mick?"

"Pretty sure, Manny. The ME's not here yet, but I'm pretty sure. It looks like he took a header down the basement stairs." Millian's voice drifted away from the line as he glanced at the body.

"So... you're at Avion's house right now?" Bruin asked.

"Yeah." He shuffled some notebook pages. "I'm at 165..."

"I know where it is!" Bruin snapped. "You say the ME's on her way, Mick?"

"Yeah."

"How long before she gets there?"

"Well... I guess she should be here within a half hour or so. We called her just before you."

For Bruin, there was another flash — this from that special theater of the mind that seasoned investigators keep close at hand. He wondered how Millian had found his way to the scene so quickly, without any word back to the SCCID. He made a mental note to ask him.

"Okay, Mick," said Bruin. "I'll be out there in ten minutes. Don't let the ME start without me, okay? I want to see just what you're seeing now."

"You got it."

Bruin slid the handset back on the cradle and stared out the door into the narrow hallway. He felt his pulse racing; his breath came in short, sharp bursts. This was the last thing he had expected — the very last. Suddenly, the season took on a very different meaning. Different, but not necessarily welcome.

December 18, 1980
1654 Callihan Creek Road, Santa Rosa

When Manny Bruin first stepped through the doors of the Sonoma County Criminal Investigation Division in 1966, Santa Rosa was a relatively small town, with a population of less than 35,000. It was a time when folks still knew a good deal about each other — sometimes more than they should have known. It was a safe place then. Everyone knew your name, your kids' names, and even whose unlicensed, untagged dog had pooped in which spacious, unfenced yard. But even then it was a time of change, and those who had lived there for years couldn't help but worry about it. Everything in 1960s America was shifting unpredictably, and Santa Rosa was no exception.

By mid-decade, Sonoma County was becoming famous for its "Wine Country" image. What had once been a guarded, inexpensive weekend retreat for San Franciscans was quickly becoming a terminus for rural wine tasting and the bed and breakfast stopovers that dotted the hills around town. It was the beginning of the end of a forgotten country town, although no one could have suspected how rapidly that end would come.

Fifteen years later, in 1980, Santa Rosa had blossomed to more than 95,000 souls. It wasn't a town anymore. It was a city, with the full range of niceties and absurdities that typify California cities. Still, for those who remembered when Santa Rosa was just a country town, it remained a familiar, generally comfortable place to live.

Like most long-time residents, Manny Bruin had always felt at home here, even when the quiet community was no longer so quiet. It was the price of change and, in the end, it didn't matter what anyone thought about it. It just was.

Highway 101 bisects Santa Rosa at an odd angle as it heads north, separating the East Side from the West, the "downtown" side from the rows of California-style homes that stretch westward. Near the city center, on both sides of the highway, the homes are older and well-shaded, and the businesses thrive in modest, tightly compressed storefronts along straight, aging streets. Moving away from the highway in either direction, the homes become more generous, less well-built, and more open to the elements. The small, personalized downtown shops become impersonal, sterile shopping malls. On the East Side, cars and kids and people seem to be everywhere, all at once. It was here, on Callihan Creek

Road, within a few blocks of Highway 101, where Byron Avion lived and died in a house with a history.

In 1946, the Sandypoint Construction Company began leveling two square blocks of a dry creek that lay just north of downtown Santa Rosa. This was the first flush of a construction explosion that would mark ground zero for the emerging Baby Boom generation. In those days, Highway 101 was little more than a two-lane country road meandering north to nowhere. The population of the town was a bit over 13,000.

The original owner of Sandypoint was Samuel Pinelli, a native who claimed that he could trace his Santa Rosa lineage back three generations. Because Callihan Creek was his company's first attempt at a major development, Pinelli wanted to prove a point to would-be buyers, so he staked a claim to the first home that was finished. Its address was 1654 Callihan Creek Road — Byron Avion's last residence.

In March 1947, Pinelli and his pregnant wife, Margaret, moved into their new home with substantial fanfare and one day's paid holiday for all their workers. Standing on the first corner of the first block of the new development, the Pinelli home was a taut and tidy two-bedroom of frame and stucco. It was patterned after the homes being built to the south in San Francisco, except that it offered special amenities, like a rambling backyard. What was most unique about it, though, was the huge, windowless room that Sam had constructed below ground, underneath the living and dining areas. His was the only house in the development to have such a basement, and Sam quickly turned it into a combination of architectural planning office and entertainment center. It was this secluded and comfortable space that would become Byron Avion's living quarters many years later. The narrow stairs leading down from the hallway would mark the path of his final earthly journey.

The Pinellis raised their only son, Robert, on Callihan Creek Road. They sent him off to make his way as an East Coast investment broker and eventually grew old in that house. In 1970, Sam died of a cerebral aneurysm while sitting at his desk in the downstairs room. Margaret hung on for a time but eventually realized that she couldn't live alone in a house so filled with memories. In the fall of 1971, she sold it to Jacqueline Avion, Byron's mother, and took up residence in a care facility on the West Side. The next year, she died.

Manny Bruin, who had known the Pinellis in passing, never had a good feeling about the white and brown house on Callihan Creek Road, and he certainly had little use for its current occupants, the Avions. The downstairs room that had once been Sam Pinelli's pride and joy gave him the creeps. Byron Avion had transformed it into an inner sanctum that was his and his alone. It was a place of secrets, none of which would be shared, some of which were to be feared.

As Bruin pulled his blue, 1978 Ford sedan across the mouth of the brick driveway, his mind was awash with memories of that room and its ominous occupant, Suspect Zero. As soon as the Avion house came into view, the Lieutenant felt those vacant rumblings in his stomach — that cop-sense that always put him on edge; that thrilled him and sickened him, all at once. He was stepping back in time, into the hunt of his career, the case that had gone astray and left him old before his time.

Bruin scanned the weathered house from behind the wheel of his sedan. He was thankful that he would be among friends today, Mick Millian and Cindy Turgell. In front of the residence he could see Mick's sedan, a twin to his, along with a white patrol car, aligned bumper-to-bumper at the curb. The ME's car was nowhere in sight. No medical personnel had arrived either, which struck him as unusual.

The lieutenant walked up the driveway, across the patchy brown lawn to the foot of the landing. He paused for a moment at the four concrete steps that led up to a wide, railed veranda. Beyond the half-opened front door he could hear Mick's muffled voice. The Detective was talking to someone in the front room. The other voice belonged to a woman — a middle-aged woman with a crusty, harsh timbre that he immediately recognized.

Bruin bounded up the stairs in two strides and through the vintage maple door, pushing it harder than he meant to and smashing it against the inside wall. It gave a resounding thud as he crossed the threshold, interrupting the conversation in the adjacent room. The lieutenant turned left, toward the voices, and squinted through the semi-darkness, trying to focus on the figures huddled around the high-backed couch under the draped far window. One of them turned and moved in his direction.

"Hi, Manny." The sergeant spoke in a low voice as he stepped away from the muddy dimness.

Bruin smiled and cleared his throat but said nothing. He slid silently to the right, to peer around Millian in the direction of the couch. The remaining figure was sitting on the edge of the couch with her legs tightly crossed, hands on her lap. She looked like a gaunt, aging, overdressed statue.

"Is that her?" Manny asked. "Is that Jacqueline?"

"Yeah," Millian answered. "I've been trying to find out what happened here. She's the one who discovered the body. Apparently, she got back from one of her trips this morning and found him at the bottom of the stairs. You know, Manny, she's as matter-of-fact about this as anyone I've ever seen. It's like she found a flower pot tipped over or something." He shook his head with a narrow, confused look.

"Umm..." Bruin gurgled impassively. "I'm not surprised."

"You want to talk to her?" Millian offered.

Manny shook his head sharply. "No." He pulled back a bit and stared directly at the sergeant.

"Listen, Mick, I want to see the body, alright?"

Millian tugged briefly on the lieutenant's right arm and headed down the short, narrow hallway. To the right of where they walked, steep stairs ascended to the second floor. Like those stairs, the flooring beneath their feet was deep brown, unpolished hardwood. The surrounding walls were painted a chocolate color, making the entire area seem tunnel-like and claustrophobic. Where the stairs reached a height of about seven feet, a maple doorway had been constructed in the space below. Beyond that door was another cramped stairway, this one constructed of unfinished risers, which led to the subterranean room.

Millian pulled on the dented, tarnished doorknob. The stairs here were much steeper and less maintained than the ones above. A single bulb gave out a dim and diffused light; the air rising from the room below was thick and still. Manny felt familiar knots in his stomach, took a few short breaths and quietly cleared his throat.

Millian led them cautiously downward, bracing himself alternately between a solid plaster wall to the left and a rough, wooden handrail to the right. At the bottom of the stairs lay Byron Avion, his legs draped crazily upward on the last riser, his head face down on the concrete floor. The two men stepped delicately around the body and huddled together near the dead man's head.

Bruin pulled out a stout black flashlight and worked the beam around Avion's head, leaning lower to examine the side of his face that was visible from above. The dead man's eyes were half-open, grayish-blue, expressionless and cloudy. His right temple and cheek were marked by several abrasions. To Manny, they looked like a series of scrapes – parallel wounds that had barely broken the skin. There was no bleeding and no other obvious signs of trauma to the body. The man was fully clothed, except for his feet. They were bare. The lieutenant placed two fingers on the side of Avion's face. The skin was cold to the touch.

"Has he been moved, Mick?" Bruin asked in a hushed tone.

"No... I don't think so. She said she didn't touch him. Just called us."

"So, she *never* called the EMT unit or 911?"

"Nope... interesting, eh?"

"Oh yeah, Mick. Interesting, all right. She's a real piece of work." The lieutenant stepped carefully around the body to examine it from another angle.

Behind him, from the darkness at the far end of the room, Bruin heard a scurrying sound. He snapped his head to the left and noticed that Millian was looking too, and listening intently. A fat, black, tawny squirrel raced past the lieutenant's leg, disappearing into the slit-like opening between the first and second stair.

"Jesus!" Mick gasped. "Scared the shit out of me!"

"Avion collected them... or something like that, didn't he, Mick? There are probably dozens of them down here."

"Jesus!" Mick repeated. He ignored the question and stared at the opening. The sergeant hunched his shoulders, sucked in some air, and shook his hands to get the blood running again.

Bruin slid down to his knees and tugged gently at Avion's extended right arm, which lay palm side up across the small of his back. It was not stiff and immobile as he had expected.

"How long, do you think?" he asked Millian. "How long has he been here, Mick?"

"I'm not sure, Manny. A few days... maybe less. No rigor that I could see. The old lady claims that she's been gone for over a month and no one else ever came to the house. From the looks of the body, I'd guess a few days, at the most."

"Yeah, me too," Bruin affirmed. "Me too."

Bruin stood and moved cautiously around the room, weaving the beam of his flashlight ahead of him, looking for a better source of light. Against the far wall, toward the front of the old house, he found a massive metal desk with a black armature lamp. The lieutenant worked his way over and flipped the switch, casting light across the floor of the dungeon. He could see most of the room now, and it was just as he had remembered it: cluttered, but relatively well-organized. Bruin could hear the faint scurrying of squirrels from everywhere. They were moving around in the maze of boxes, crates, and containers that covered most of the floor in neatly aligned rows. Many of the boxes had been meticulously tied with white nylon rope. Still, there were plenty of places between the boxes for a squirrel to hide. Glancing at his partner, Bruin could see that Mick heard them too; his eyes darted back and forth, trying to follow the scraping sounds.

"God, Manny, do those things carry a disease or something? What happens if they bite you?"

Bruin laughed and hunched his shoulders. He didn't know.

"I'm looking for two men and a stiff," came a singsong voice.

Manny chuckled and nodded knowingly at Millian. The diminutive, red-haired, middle-aged woman standing at the top of the stairs was Dr. Cynthia Turgell, the Sonoma County Medical Examiner. She had joined the ME's office a decade earlier, in 1970, as the Assistant Medical Examiner. Two years later, she took over the chief's post when the incumbent, Howard Vorhies, retired after more than twenty years on the job. Cynthia was the first woman to hold that position, and her early days were rough. In time, she proved herself in a big way, even in the male-dominated, locker-room environment of the SCCID. Turgell had a sixth sense that the law enforcement community respected. Better still, she was a team player, who worked hard to keep her name out of the papers and throw the credit to others. She was one of them now, and when Cindy Turgell spoke, the investigators listened.

"Come on down and join us, Cindy," Mick replied. "And the damn squirrels."

Turgell snorted something that sounded like "squirrels" as she worked her way down the stars. The three of them stared at Avion's corpse. Turgell scanned the area.

"So..." she hummed, nodding her head up and down. "Here lies your infamous pal, Suspect Zero, eh? He doesn't look like so much now, does he?"

Bruin nodded slowly but said nothing. The doctor pulled out a pair of flesh-colored latex gloves and snapped them over her thin fingers. She knelt next to the head of the corpse and ran a finger along the side of the dead man's face. With her left hand, she jabbed at the flesh around his jawbone and throat.

"He's been here for a few days, Manny. That's for sure... the cellar kept him cool... kept him in good shape..." Turgell's voice trailed off as she began extracting the tools of her trade from what looked like a cheap, red plastic tackle box. It was obvious that the ME was anxious to get to work.

"Well, at least he doesn't stink yet," she mumbled.

Bruin shook his head in tight little jerks. His humor tank had already run dry and he had never been a fan of the coroner's trade. It was time to get out of the basement.

"Listen, Cindy, we're going upstairs to talk to his mother, alright?"

"Umm..." was all she said, as she examined Avion's right arm.

"Call us if there's anything, will you?"

"Umm..." She pulled on the wrist and fingers of Avion's right hand.

Bruin and Millian stepped cautiously over the dead man's legs and made their way up the stairs. Halfway up, Manny stopped.

"Cindy, what about those scratches on the side of his head there? What about those?"

"Yeah, I saw those, Manny," she answered without looking up. "Looks like he may have hit his head and face on the way down, although I can't be sure." She raised her arm over her head and jabbed at the wall along the stairs.

The Lieutenant squeezed past Millian and moved carefully back down, scanning the unfinished wall where Turgell was gesturing. He flipped on the flashlight and found faint streaks of blood on the rough plaster. It looked as if Avion had hit his head against the wall about four steps above the floor. From there, he must have spun as he fell and crashed down across the last riser. At least, it looked that way.

"Yeah, okay..." Bruin said. "Good catch."

"Umm..." she hummed back. "That's one for me."

Bruin thought for a moment, still staring at the streaks. "So, you're telling me that he hit his head on the wall and then fell down the stairs?"

"No, not necessarily, Manny. I didn't say that. I don't know yet. My guess is that he was dead by the time he hit the bottom stair, though. There's almost no bleeding from these wounds." She poked again at the side of Avion's head.

"Okay, Cindy, we'll be back." Bruin turned to face Millian and waved him up the stairs. They worked their way to the darkened living room where Jacqueline Avion waited motionless on the couch. Millian stood back and let Bruin move in closer. Their routines were practiced and precise, perfected by years of working together.

"Mrs. Avion, do you remember me?" the lieutenant asked the old woman. Her face was cast down, her eyes aimlessly working around the intricate blue and pink floral patterns of the rug. She made no movement at all.

"Yes," she answered, in a deep monotone.

"Can you tell me what happened here? What happened with your son?"

"He died... obviously," she snapped. "I've already told Sergeant Millian about it."

Bruin shrugged his shoulders in Millian's direction and gently sat down next to her. He looked intently at her rigid, unpleasant profile, waiting for some kind of response. There was none — just the frail, impassive outline against the darkness of the room.

"Did you find him, Mrs. Avion?" Bruin asked.

"Yes."

"When?"

"A few hours ago... when I got back."

"Back from where?"

"A trip. I was in South American on a trip," she said passively. "I always travel in the winter."

Bruin looked up at the sergeant, who was standing a few feet away. As their eyes met, Millian tilted his head to the right, as if to say, "I told you so." It was obvious that Jacqueline Avion had little to say. She knew nothing, or at least wanted them to believe that.

"All right, Mrs. Avion, I just have one more question, then I'll leave you alone."

The woman let out a hollow sigh and nodded her head.

"You didn't like Byron very much, did you? You didn't like your son?" Bruin sat back, expecting an onslaught that would bring her out — hoping for some kind of reaction. No such luck.

"Not very much," she whispered. "Just like everyone else, Lieutenant. Just like you. Not very much."

Millian stepped forward to get Bruin's attention. He motioned toward his own chest with a cupped right hand, silently asking the lieutenant to join him. Bruin pushed away from the couch and stood in front of the sergeant, with his back turned to protect their conversation. He needn't have bothered. She was still lost amid the flowers on the rug.

"The ME's wagon is here, Manny," Millian whispered, nodding his head to the front door.

Bruin turned around and stared at Mrs. Avion, hoping that she would offer a bit more, but still there was nothing. He decided it didn't matter. He had had enough of her.

"Sergeant Millian has a few more questions and a form to fill out, Mrs. Avion. Please cooperate with him," the lieutenant ordered.

Bruin didn't bother to wait for a response. He strode quickly past the sergeant and back down the hallway toward the descending stairs. Standing at the top of the stairs, he could see Cindy Turgell still working on Avion's body. Somehow, she had managed to turn the 230-pound frame onto its back. He had wondered more than once how she managed to do that kind of thing.

"Well, Cindy?" he asked. "Anything?"

"I think it's a natural, Manny. No evidence of foul play that I can see. I'm going to need an autopsy and some forensic work to confirm that, though. Do we need someone's okay for the autopsy?"

"Yeah. Mick's going to take care of that. He's doing it now. No problem. You'll have what you need in a few minutes."

"Okay, Manny. Is the wagon here yet?"

"Yeah. They're out front. They're waiting for you to release the scene."

"Okay, good," she chirped, and stood, ripping the latex gloves from her hands and stuffing them into the tackle box. "Let's haul him out of here and I'll get right on it."

"When?" the lieutenant asked.

"I'll have something for you by tomorrow afternoon, Manny. Come on over in the afternoon, alright?"

"Yep, perfect, Cindy. Tomorrow afternoon. Thanks."

December 19, 1980
Sonoma County Medical Examiner's Office

The Lieutenant sat across the smooth metal table as Cindy Turgell fingered her way through Byron Avion's last official file. Bruin could see the business end of the Medical Examiner's office through a wide, thick plate glass window. Two stainless steel examining tables sat in the center of the room, dominating everything else. Around the walls stood a variety of sinks, cabinets, trays with implements whose names were unpronounceable, and dozens of containers with labels even more mysterious. Bruin was uncomfortable in this place. He squirmed in a pink plastic chair that was too small for his frame.

"So," Turgell began, "Do you want the English version?"

"Please." He gave her a squeamish look.

"All right. We diced him, we sliced him, and we sucked him dry..."

"Jesus!" said Manny. "Give me a break!"

Turgell laughed and rested her hand on his arm.

"Sorry, Manny... Maybe I've just been at this too long."

He nodded, offering a stiff smile.

"I don't have all the blood work or tox-screen stuff back yet, but it was probably a natural death. He blew an artery big-time,

Manny. He was probably dead before he hit the floor. Now, there may be some stuff in the lab work that I haven't seen, so this isn't final. But, my guess is that it was a natural, subject to a few other oddities."

She sat back and waited for her guest to ask the obvious question, but he never did. Instead, Bruin just nodded and looked beyond her, fixated by the cold, clean tables in the next room. He wasn't surprised by what the ME had said. He just wanted to get the hell out of there.

"Where's his body now?" the lieutenant asked.

"He's in the bin, waiting for some kind of disposition. I suppose you're going to arrange that with the next of kin?"

"Yeah... well, Mick will. Cindy, is there anything else? Can you tell me more, or is that it?"

"Not much about the body or the man himself, Manny. He was overweight, a smoker, bad lungs, bad kidneys. From the looks of what I saw, this guy did it all to excess. He could have blown an artery at any time."

"Any sign of drugs?"

"Nothing out of the ordinary. I need the blood work to know for sure, but nothing jumped out at me."

"Any evidence of sexual activity?"

"Nope. But his prostate looked like a zeppelin. It was cancerous."

"Geez..." the Lieutenant grumbled, trying not to look down at his crotch. He continued to stare off into the examining room, feeling her eyes on him. Turgell finally decided to make an offering.

"Well, I guess this is your Christmas present, Manny? Putting Suspect Zero in the bag must feel pretty good."

Bruin snapped his head around and stared at her. His face was pale and twisted in anger, his eyes strained and frozen. Turgell slid back in her chair, but was stopped by the plate glass behind her.

"Death is no goddamn Christmas present, Cindy! Not even *his*," Bruin shouted. He pounded his finger on Avion's file.

"God, Manny, I'm..."

"This is no fucking present!" He ripped his gaze away from Turgell, threw himself from the chair and stormed out of her office, leaving his friend's heart knocking uncontrollably.

"Jesus..." she mumbled. "He didn't even let me get to the best part."

A Call from the City

By the Spring of 1971, the entire San Francisco Bay Area was in a state of siege, held hostage by the killer who called himself "Zodiac." This widespread panic included Manny Bruin's usually quiet home turf, even though the area had been spared any direct bloodshed. All they knew was that Zodiac bragged about a number of unnamed victims in his letters to the *Chronicle,* and that there was always a backlog of unsolved homicides that seemed to substantiate his words.

Zodiac's reign of terror began just before Christmas in 1968, although no one would become aware of his presence until the following summer. On December 20th, an unseen assailant slaughtered two high school teenagers while they were parked in a darkened lover's lane in Vallejo, east of San Francisco. Betty Lou Jensen and David Faraday, who were out on their first date, were shot and killed late that night. The crime scene provided virtually no clues; there were no eyewitnesses and no one came forward to claim credit for the crime. Because the two teenagers were well-regarded and had no known enemies, the investigators on the Vallejo Police Department believed that they were working a senseless, random double homicide — an event unlikely to be repeated. They would soon learn that this crime actually signaled the beginning of one of America's most notorious serial murder cases.

Six months later, early on the morning of July 5, 1969, the killer struck again. This time, he shot another couple in a deserted parking lot about two miles from the attack on Jensen and Faraday. That night, Darlene Ferrin was killed. Her friend, Michael Mageau, was seriously wounded but survived. Shortly after the shooting, an unidentified man telephoned the Vallejo Police Department and claimed credit for the assault, and also for the double homicide in December.

A little more than two weeks later, the killer wrote a series of three letters to Bay Area newspapers, and included a cryptogram that supposedly held the key to his identity. When the code was broken by a husband-and-wife team from the South Bay, it proved to be nothing more than a ruse. Zodiac had no intention of giving up his true identity so easily. This taunting communication proved to be the first of some two-dozen letters and greeting cards that would be sent to the media over the next ten years. By the end of 1969, the phrase "this is the Zodiac speaking," which is how the murderer began his letters, would become known to virtually every resident of the San Francisco Bay Area and countless others across the nation.

On September 27, 1969, Zodiac attacked for a third time at Lake Berryessa in Napa County, north of San Francisco and just east of Sonoma County. In a brutal stabbing rampage on another young couple, the fugitive claimed the life of Cecelia Sheperd and wounded her friend, Bryan Hartnell. This time, the killer planned his attack even more carefully, including an element of terror. When he confronted the couple, he wore a black executioner's hood emblazoned across the breastplate with a white cross-hair symbol. Because of this disguise, the surviving victim was never able to provide investigators with a good description. Once again, the crime scene yielded little evidence, although there was an intriguing footprint or two that seemed to have been made by a work or military-style boot.

The following month, on October 11, Zodiac broke with his pattern of attacking couples and murdered a male taxicab driver in San Francisco. He shot the driver at point-blank range in the back of his head from the rear passenger seat of the cabby's vehicle. Moments after the shooting, the killer was confronted by responding San Francisco Police Department officers but managed to talk his way out of suspicion (the patrolmen had been given an inaccurate description of the individual thought to have been connected with the incident). The officers were later able to produce a reasonably detailed sketch of the man they had met that night; however, like everything else that became connected with Zodiac, this apparently strong lead proved to be inconsequential.

Following the murders in September and October, Zodiac wrote a series of letters to the San Francisco *Chronicle,* bragging about his cruel exploits. Some of them included swatches of bloodied cloth ripped from the murdered taxicab driver's shirt. The killer threatened to blow up school buses filled with children or randomly shoot youngsters on public streets.

The result of the letters' publication was to throw the Bay Area into a state of panic. For some time, police vehicles routinely tagged along after school buses as they made their daily rounds. Off-duty law enforcement officers were regularly dispatched to ride along with the children as they traveled to and from school. Parents were outraged, and fear seemed to permeate the entire metropolitan area.

Needless to say, reports about Zodiac were regular features in newspapers, on the radio, and on television. Speculation about the unknown killer was wild and unremitting. Investigators were barraged with useless tips, demands for action, and the public release of more and more information. Columnists and commentators added to the confusion, and politicians jumped on the bandwagon at every opportunity. An army of investigators was assembled from across the Bay Area, although they were often reluctant to share information. Several careers were made while others were broken, sometimes in a heartbeat.

Throughout the remainder of 1969, Zodiac continued to write to the newspapers while the combined investigative forces of the Vallejo, Napa, and San Francisco Police departments found themselves no closer to their prey. Although there were a few physical descriptions of Zodiac, they proved to be too general to be of practical use. The crime scenes were virtually devoid of useful clues and the number of potentially viable suspects in the case quickly grew to more than 2,500, based mostly on uninformed tips from the public. In truth, investigators were stumped. To make matters worse, Zodiac had proved himself to be a master of media manipulation. He was openly taunting his adversaries and doing a magnificent job of it.

Zodiac continued to write to the *Chronicle* throughout 1970, regularly claiming more victims but never providing hard evidence of his alleged exploits. However, he kept upping the ante of death and fear with hand-scrawled "scorecards" appended to many of his missives. Although investigators could only directly attribute five murders and two injuries to Zodiac, he eventually claimed to have killed more than three-dozen victims. The overwhelming difficulty for investigators lay in the fact that the San Francisco Bay Area experienced a number of unsolved homicides during this period, and no one was sure whether or not they could be attributed to the Zodiac.

In general, investigators were divided into two camps. Some believed that Zodiac was telling the truth and that he had killed many more individuals than had been officially credited to him. Others believed that the serial killer was just bragging and had claimed no victims after October 1969. Even the pattern of the unsolved homicides in the Bay Area caused more confusion than enlightenment. Some investigators argued that the dissimilarity of the unsolved cases proved that Zodiac could not have been the perpetrator. Others pointed out that Zodiac himself had warned the public that he would change his methods of killing so as to confuse his pursuers. This, they argued, was indirect proof that he had, in fact, claimed many more victims than was officially acknowledged by investigators. In the end, no one was sure. Everyone seemed to have a theory and no one had the facts to back it up, including the killer himself. In this bigger-than-life war between good and evil, Zodiac was ahead by a few touchdowns, and pulling away.

It was in the midst of this ongoing chaos that Manny Bruin became involved in the Zodiac investigation. With an unexpected, unsolicited telephone call, he moved from the sidelines to the playing field in a gruesome game that he had never expected, and never wanted, to play.

May 7, 1971
SCCID Office

The call came in 1971, from a man who was quickly becoming a Bay Area legend — Sam Lionell. Whether that legend would turn out to be good or bad was still up for debate, although knowledgeable folks would have bet on the plus side. Regardless, no one could deny that Lionell became a genuine and enduring San Francisco celebrity, as well as the one man who truly understood the failed public investigation. It was the Zodiac case that ensured Lionell's place in history — and ruined his health.

Tall, dusky, stylish, articulate, and nothing short of brilliant, Lionell was the epitome of a successful big-city homicide detective. With his charm and good looks, the Inspector was also a natural draw for the media. He was a man who knew how to close a homicide case with speed and flair. He had a long history of bringing his man to justice while still managing to look more like a Wall Street executive than a flatfoot. Lionell was a perennial front-page favorite, a cultural icon whose quotes were often the fare of late edition headlines. It didn't hurt that he was also savvy and well-connected.

By the winter of 1970, however, Lionell was deep into the Zodiac case, and clearly frustrated by it. The killer had managed to walk away from a series of brutal, risky crimes with uncanny ease. He had proven his ability to manipulate the press and, frankly, he was making investigators look bad. This kind of affair did not please Lionell, who took justifiable pride in his long string of successes. Now, in early 1971, SFPD investigators found themselves resigned to working as many public tips as possible, no matter how far-fetched, simply because they had run out of anything more promising. For the past several months, each tip seemed to draw them further from the center of the case rather than closer to their prey. Still, Lionell understood that this was the best course at hand, especially given the lack of hard evidence, and in

March he finally came across a piece of information that seemed promising.

Sally Ventable, Byron Avion's ebony-haired, twenty-seven-year-old cousin, had called Inspector Lionell with a story that tweaked the investigator's antennae. Sally recounted a series of strange events that, taken together, led her to believe that her cousin might be the infamous Zodiac. On the face of it, there was nothing especially unusual about her story. She certainly wasn't the first tipster to call and point a finger at a disfavored relative. Sally, however, was particularly convincing, both in her obvious concern and in her ability to back up her ideas with interesting factual tidbits.

The immediate problem was that Cousin Byron didn't fit the physical bill all that well, and that had become a key part of the Zodiac investigation. In fact, after the two SFPD officers had unwittingly spoken to Zodiac following the taxicab murder, they had provided a reasonably detailed description. It was this description that the SFPD had come to rely on. As it turned out, Cousin Byron was a bit too large and a bit too old. But those descriptions in the Zodiac file had always troubled Lionell. They were just too different from each other in small ways, too vague to be trusted. For the moment, he was willing to overlook them if he found something better.

Ventable reported seeing a large, bloody knife in Avion's car shortly after the Lake Berryessa attack in September 1969. From her description, it seemed to closely match the weapon investigators believed the attacker had used on his young victims. After she noticed the knife, Cousin Byron became rather agitated, made some feeble excuse about the blood on the blade, and arranged to have it disappear — forever.

Then there was the matter of speech. Sally's cousin often used phraseology that was hauntingly reminiscent of Zodiac's letters. Moreover, according to Sally, he was very fond of cryptography and cryptograms, just like Zodiac. It was an interest and a skill that he had picked up in the military. Also, no one in the family was apparently able to account for Byron's whereabouts on the dates of the crimes. Sally made a special point to note this fact in her conversation with Lionell.

Further, Avion had often spoken about his cousin of his fascination with the Zodiac, and had even wondered aloud if he was a suspect. Sally considered this interest unhealthy and unusual. Lionell was skeptical.

Sally added a baggage car full of little things: similar handwriting, a virtual storehouse of stuff hidden in cardboard boxes, three different cars, several different residences, a fascination with romantic couples, secret journals in coded handwriting, and mysterious comings and goings. By the end of their two-hour conversation, the pragmatic, cynical cop was convinced that this was a lead worth pursuing. Sally's enthusiasm was infectious and, besides, the inspector had little else to inspect.

At the time of the Ventable call, Byron Avion had two known addresses. His primary residence was at his mother's house in San Francisco, in an area known as Potrero Hill. However, he also rented a tiny apartment in Santa Rosa, very close to the junior college where he took classes. Avion's cousin had described him as a perpetual student with no specific educational goal. She also mentioned that his Santa Rosa apartment was strictly off-limits, to friends and family alike. He guarded its sanctity meticulously. She had no idea what he did in that apartment, but she was sure that it was unhealthy.

Avion worked a series of odd jobs, both in the City and in Sonoma County, to keep himself afloat. He was often ill-tempered, angry, always secretive, and a dedicated loner. All in all, according to Sally, this man looked like a good candidate for the role of a serial killer. Besides that, he was a royal pain in the ass, and she had grown to fear him.

Although the detective was careful to play it loose and easy with his tipster, Lionell agreed that Byron Avion was an interesting possibility. Now he needed to make an important decision – what to do with this information; how to use it in such a way that would not jeopardize the reputation of what would probably turn out to be an innocent man with a collection of quirky habits. Still, there was always the other possibility, and to Sam Lionell's way of thinking, it was worth a little effort to play it out. He needed to call a comrade up north; he needed some good contacts in Sonoma County.

He needed Manny Bruin.

"Manny! It's been a while," Lionell yelped into the line. "It's been a *long* while..."

"Yep, it sure has," the detective replied, trying to recall when the two had lost spoken. "But I've been keeping up on you, Sam. You're face is all over the papers and TV. Guess you've been busy down there?" It wasn't a question; it was a gentle poke in the side. Everyone knew that the Zodiac investigation was on life-support.

"Well..." Sam paused, considering his answer. This was a fellow fraternity member, so the direct approach was usually the best. "To tell the truth, I'm busy going nowhere, I guess. This Zodiac thing is giving me a major ulcer, Manny, and that's no joke. I'm up to my eyeballs in shit and down to working every tip that sounds anywhere in the ballpark. Anyway, there's no point in crying about it. I've got something here that I need your help with."

"Sure. Glad to help." Bruin was curious but tried hard not to show it. He liked Lionell. But he never socialized with the big city detective and really didn't know the man well. What he did know was that Sam was desperately trying to hold the reins on a sensational case, and that was more than enough to get Manny's attention.

"Okay, here's the deal," Lionell began. "This woman called me because she's convinced that her cousin is the Zodiac. Now, before you tell me where to get off, I've got a feeling about this one, Manny. She had a lot of good information. It all fit well — maybe too well. At any rate, I want to work this one out and I need your help."

"Sure, Sam. Whatever. Give me the details." Bruin knew exactly what Lionell meant. There was always that *feeling*. It wasn't always right, but it was something that no good investigator could ignore.

"Good! The guy's name is Byron Avion and he has an apartment up near Santa Rosa Junior College. His primary residence is here in the City. He lives with his mother. He's been spending a lot of time up your way, for months, and I want to get in and look at his place. There's no way I can get a search warrant for the City address since it belongs to his mother, but I've got a good shot at the one in Sonoma County, if I can get you to put it in front of the right judge and be a part of the search. You up for that?"

"Byron Avion..." Manny paused, his mind shuffling through a catalog of names and faces. This guy wasn't familiar. "Well, sure, Sam. I don't see why not. You think this guy is a good suspect? Does he have a record?'

Lionell went quiet.

"No record.   And, well... no... I have no *good* reason to consider him a suspect, Manny. It's a feeling. You know how that works."

"Alright, Sam," the detective answered. "I can understand where you're at on this. I'm happy to help. How do you want to work it?"

"I'll get someone to courier up the file on this guy, along with the warrant request." Lionell's voice was animated and enthusiastic. "If you can make this work in front of a judge up your way, call me and we'll talk to Avion and search the place. We'll work him together. You all right with that?"

"Yeah, I'm fine with that, Sam. Send it up. I'll get right on it."

June 4, 1971
37441 College Way South, Apartment 17A

It had taken much too long to get the search warrant, and Sam Lionell had been on the phone to Bruin nearly every day for updates. He was anxious to follow up on this one, and the slow-moving, cautious Sonoma County legal system was beginning to frustrate him. For Manny, getting the damn warrant had taken five trips to the courthouse, two different judges, and a lot of fast-talking. In truth, there was no good reason to suspect Byron Avion in the Zodiac case; there was nothing to link him to the investigation, except for what his cousin had told Sam Lionell. The search warrant application listed a hodgepodge of items that *could* be connected to Zodiac, but none of them were precise or necessarily related to Byron Avion. In fact, it was a strange and eclectic list of goodies that could belong to anyone: a large hunter's knife with a carved handle, handguns of a specific caliber, black cloth, a sewing machine, books on bomb-making and cryptography, blank sheets of vellum of a certain size, a specific type of felt tip pen, copies of San Francisco *Examiner* articles of certain dates, and a long list of other household items that seemed pretty innocuous. For Sam Lionell, though, the one magic item in this list was a request to collect samples of the suspect's handwriting. If Lionell could match that handwriting sample to one or more of Zodiac's letters, he'd have the start of a great case.

The first judge to study the warrant application expressed a good deal of legitimate concern about invading the privacy of a citizen on such slim cause. It all seemed too fast and loose. For the conservative, seventy-three-year-old Santa Rosa resident, this worry enough to throw out the request, despite Bruin's arguments that Avion was a potentially strong suspect in multiple murders. The second judge, however, proved to be more reluctant about throwing up a roadblock. He was not about to take the blame for letting a potential suspect walk away from the sensational Zodiac case. He was also a much younger man, who kept one eye on the law and the other on his career. Avion's rights became a secondary issue, and the warrant was approved.

With the signed warrant in hand, the investigators set a date to visit Mr. Avion. They would approach their suspect on one of the days that he attended classes at the local junior college. They would take him as he left his apartment, walk him back in, search the place, and get some handwriting samples.

Four days later, Bruin and Lionell sat in the front seat of Bruin's blue sedan with Millian in the back, directly across the street from Byron Avion's low-budget apartment house. They quietly scanned the entranceway to the building and the open area next to it. It was early-morning, about an hour before Avion was scheduled to leave for class, and they wanted to be sure that their man was still inside the apartment before they made their move.

Lionell was especially anxious that this search go right the first time. He was convinced that they would probably never get a second shot. What they had in hand was just too fuzzy to try and drag it before another judge, and there was no chance of ever getting a search warrant for Mrs. Avion's house in San Francisco. This would be it, so they had better get it right.

"Have you seen these?" Sam asked Bruin. Lionell flipped open the pliant, thick flap of a black leather folio, took out several photocopies, and offered them to Manny.

The Detective studied each page, holding them closer to the windshield to make maximum use of the gray morning light.

Although the pages were a bit muddy and wrinkled, it was obvious that he was holding copies of Zodiac's letters to the San Francisco *Chronicle*, a newspaper in Vallejo, the Los Angeles *Times*, and one strange, pleading missive that had been written to San Francisco attorney Melvin Belli. Each sheet had been carefully marked and dated with an SFPD evidence stamp. In all, Bruin counted more than a dozen pages.

Portions of a few of the letters had been reprinted in the San Francisco *Chronicle* over the last two years. Manny recognized the disjointed scrawl and strange phraseology. However, a few of the letters had never made it to a newspaper, or anywhere else outside the SFPD. Manny looked at these with extra care.

"These are all the letters?" Manny asked. "I mean, these are all his? Zodiac's?"

"Yeah," Lionell muttered, staring out the passenger's window at the apartment building. "There are one or two that aren't there, but that's most of them." His tone was evasive and distant. It didn't leave room for a follow-up question. Manny was convinced that there were letters missing from this stack. He just wasn't sure if it was important enough to risk pissing off his guest.

Bruin reshuffled his way through the stack, taking time to examine each copy as carefully as he could. With this second pass, he focused on the handwriting. In some cases it was stilted and uneven, each sentence ending lower than where it had begun. In others, like the Belli letter, the handwriting was square, measured

— as if it had been written by a third-grade teacher on a blackboard. At least two of the letters contained line drawings of some kind of explosive devices. Two others had coded messages — strange cryptograms with characters that looked like backward letters, regular letters, and astrological symbols. Then Sam tugged at his arm.

"Manny, these are the key," he said in a confidential voice. "If we can match Avion to these letters — if we can match his handwriting — I might have something going here. These are very important..." He looked away, toward the apartment, before finishing his thought

"Oh, by the way, Manny. This guy has an IQ in the high 130s, so nothing would surprise me... nothing. He's ambidextrous. He's brilliant. He's a piece of work..." Lionell mumbled. "We need to be careful..."

The detective listened but said nothing. Lionell had drifted off somewhere. Bruin fingered the photocopy on the top of the stack and slid it onto his left thigh to keep it in sight. He pulled the next page close to it and tried to examine the handwriting side-by-side. The two letters seemed to be very different, although they could have been written with the same instrument. It was hard to tell from the copies. Bruin examined a third letter. It was different from the first two, although the handwriting did have some similarities.

"Listen, Sam, I'm no handwriting expert, but some of these look different. I mean, if these were written by the same guy, how come the styles are so different? Look at this one to Melvin Belli, then look at some of the others." He pushed the single page from his thigh back onto the stack, ready to hand them back to Sam.

Lionell cleared his throat and reached for them without looking at Bruin. "Yeah, I had a problem with that too, at first. These were checked out, though. They were cleared in Sacramento. They were written by the same guy. They're all his."

Sam stuffed the copies back into the folio and snapped the leather flap closed. It was obvious that he didn't want to discuss it anymore. He wanted to get down to business. Bruin began to wonder why Sam had even bothered to show him the letters in the first place, but the thought was interrupted.

"Manny," Millian whispered from the back seat. "That's our guy coming down the walkway, isn't it?"

Bruin glanced past Lionell and peered out the passenger window. Moving quickly in their direction was a large, stocky man dressed in a dark blue windbreaker zipped up to the neck, black pants, and heavy work boots. He had short-cropped, receding hair and was wearing glasses with staunch, black rims. His walk was metered and determined, almost stiff. The man had tied the cuffs of his pants around the top of his boots with thin, white nylon rope. It was Byron Avion.

As he strode down the walkway from the apartment building, he moved his head rapidly back and forth, taking in everything as he made his way to the street. Without speaking, Bruin and Lionell pushed open their respective doors and moved quickly toward Avion, with Mick in tow. It was Manny who reached him first, just as he turned left to where his white 1962 Chevy sedan was parked on the street.

"Mr. Avion? Byron Avion?" Bruin announced from a distance of three feet. Avion took a step backward but did not turn. He stopped, stood rigidly at attention, and stared at the detective for several seconds before canvassing the other two men who had formed a semicircle in front of him.

"Yeah," he said in a halting, flat voice. "Yeah... what do you want?"

Bruin noticed that Avion had stuck his hands in his jacket pockets.

"I'm Detective Bruin," Manny began, whipping out his SCCID identification and badge. "This is Inspector Lionell and Detective Millian," he continued without taking his eyes off Avion. "Please take your hands out of your pockets so I can see them. We'd like to talk to you for a few moments."

Avion's face turned from stone, to passive, to a deep scowl, to a tight, teasing smile, all in a matter of seconds. He slowly withdrew his hands from each pocket and showed them to the detective, palms up, in a mocking gesture of surrender. With that final, theatrical flair, Manny could almost picture a light bulb going off over the cropped, light brown hair. He was enjoying this!

"Oh, sure," Avion continued, speaking directly to Bruin. "I expected you. Are we going to do this downtown or right here on the street?"

"We're going to do it here! Right here!" Lionell snapped, stepping to a few inches from the large man's face. "No... In fact, we're going to do it inside." He jabbed an angry finger toward the apartment building.

Avion turned to face Lionell and scanned him from head to toe. He finished the examination with a deep stare into his eyes.

"You're from the SFPD, aren't you?" Avion asked with a smirk. "Your face is all over the *Chronicle* these days. You're just a little guy, aren't you?"

Lionell was ready to explode. His mouth fell open, his jaw quivered, but he was too angry to make a sound.

"All right, Mr. Avion, that's enough!" Bruin interrupted, trying to keep the situation in hand. "Let's finish this conversation inside your apartment. Or, if you like, we can do it elsewhere." The threat was obvious.

Lionell nodded vigorously but wisely said nothing.

"I don't think so!" Avion shot back. "I don't think so... unless you have a search warrant?"

Without speaking, Manny pulled the warrant from his inside jacket pocket and pushed it in Avion's direction. Avion didn't bother to read it but just stuffed it into the pocket of his windbreaker with a snarl.

"Yeah, all right. Let's get on with it," Avion grumbled. He turned to move back up the walkway toward his first-floor apartment. "I know why you're here, so let's get it over with. I've got shit to do today and you're not part of my plans."

To call Byron Avion's apartment a "residence" would be like calling those cracks in the sidewalk "ravines." His place was nothing more than a room that had once been a storage area for the other apartments in the building — no more than 350 square feet, including an afterthought of a kitchen slung into the east end. It was located on the ground floor in the back, at the base of a two-story apartment building that had been thrown together in the typical style of the early 1960s construction frenzy. The apartment was much smaller than the surrounding units and windowless on three walls. The only natural light came from an undersized, shuttered window that had been hacked into the wall just above a feeble excuse for a kitchen sink. The floor was carpeted in a matted, blue-green shag that exuded a musty, dense odor permeating the room. The undecorated walls had been covered with several coats of semi-gloss paint whose color attempted to match that of the carpet but failed by several shades of green. The result of this overbearing pea-soup environment was to give the unit an oppressive, almost nauseating feel, as if one had just stepped off a salmon trawler in the middle of February.

What little furniture that existed looked as if it belonged on a low-budget Hollywood movie set from the 1930s. Two rickety mahogany chairs had been pushed up against the west end. Nearby, a sheetless, blanketless mattress had been thrown on the floor. In the middle of the room sat a tiny, square end table made of nondescript blonde wood. With these few exceptions, the apartment was bare.

First through the door on the heels of the brusque tenant, Bruin took one step inside and immediately began rubbing his nose with the back of his hand. It was the most bizarre living arrangement — or lack of arrangement — that the Detective had ever seen. He could tell from the pale, drawn expression on Sam Lionell's face that this was not what he had expected, either. Lionell grabbed Bruin by the arm and swung him around, positioning him so that the Detective's back was to Avion.

"Listen, Manny, there's something wrong here. Something's very wrong. Nobody lives like this," he whispered.

Manny nodded his head and gave a slight shrug of his shoulders.

"I want to look around, Manny. Will you talk to him?"

"Sure."

"Let's get this done!" Avion yelped. "I've got to get going sometime before the end of the year!"

"All right, Mr. Avion," Manny answered in a low voice, turning toward him. "Inspector Lionell will take a quick look around." He waited for some response. There was none. By then, Lionell had begun his search.

Bruin walked across the room, past Avion, and pulled one of the rickety chairs from the wall. He motioned for Avion to do the same. The big man just smiled and sat down where he had been standing, cross-legged on the carpet. Manny sat down in the chair, keeping a careful distance. From behind Avion he could see Millian quietly close the door to the apartment and station himself in front of it. He rested his right hand on the handle of the .38 in his belt. He looked troubled and uneasy, scanning the room with his eyes.

"Mr. Avion," Bruin began matter-of-factly, "you said you were expecting us, didn't you?"

"That's what I said."

"Why was that? Why were you expecting us?"

"You think I'm the Zodiac killer, that's why. You've been tipped that I'm the guy you're looking for. You think I'm *the man*..." His face grew bright and animated.

"Why do you say that, Mr. Avion?"

"Oh, come on," he snapped. "I'm not fucking stupid!" Avion turned and watched Sam Lionell poking through the only closet in the room. It was located on the west wall, near the mattress on the floor, and was barely wide enough to stand in. There were a few articles of clothing on hangers and a single cardboard box on the floor. It had been tied tightly with thin, white cord to keep it closed. Lionell had pulled the box out of the closet, untied the knots, and was squatting on one knee over it, rummaging through the contents.

"You're going to be very disappointed," Avion announced to Lionell's back in a falsetto voice. "You're not going to find anything you want, Little Man."

Lionell grumbled something angry as he worked his way through the contents of the box. Old school books, a few faded blue shirts, some pieces of linen, plastic knives and forks, nothing.

"Well... are you a killer?" Bruin whispered at the man on the floor, trying to regain his attention. "Are you Zodiac? Are you *the man*?" It wasn't subtle, but it was worth a try. Besides, this guy was pissing him off.

Avion roared with laughter and shook his head from side to side, tears running down his full, flushed cheeks. Manny scanned Avion's face, looking for any sign of discomfort, looking for a reason. There was nothing to see. This guy was enjoying his "unexpected" visit and had gone fishing with them. What little anger he showed struck Bruin as feigned. He *liked* what was happening here. He *was* expecting it.

Lionell threw the articles back into the cardboard box and angrily slid it into the closet. He walked across the room and began searching the drawers in the kitchen area. With the exception of a few household items, they were bare. The tiny cupboard above and to the right of the sink held only a single, dirty glass. Frustrated, Lionell whipped around and jumped to the center of the room, putting himself between Bruin and Avion. His face was twisted and enraged.

"You son-of-a-bitch, you don't live here!" the Inspector screamed. "Where do you live? Where do you live!" His right arm was cocked above Avion's head in a threatening gesture, his fist tight and ready. Bruin jumped from the chair and grabbed Lionell's arm. Avion sat motionless, looking up at Lionell with a beaming smirk. Suddenly, it turned dark and ominous.

"Fuck you, Shorty!" said the big man.

Bruin could feel the Inspector's arm move forward, struggling against the restraint. He was furious. Manny motioned at Millian for some help. Mick jumped forward and stood close to Lionell.

"Listen, I think you and the inspector should take a look at Mr. Avion's car," Bruin said, still pulling on the inspector's arm. Lionell got the message. He relaxed his arm.

"Yeah, good idea," the inspector said. He spun past Avion and headed for the apartment door with Millian in tow.

Avion jumped to his feet, ripped the search warrant from his jacket pocket, and began to unfold it.

"Wait a minute!" he screamed. "You have no right to search my car! Let me read this." He waved the warrant at their backs. He tried to move after them but Manny yanked at the collar of his windbreaker, keeping him in place.

Lionell turned briefly as he moved across the threshold and gave Avion another enraged stare. "Fuck you!" he grumbled and slammed the apartment door so hard that it bounced against the frame and swung open. Avion pulled angrily toward the door, trying to break Bruin's grip on his collar.

"All right, Mr. Avion, just calm down!" Manny ordered, yanking on the taller man. "Calm down!" he shouted. Avion eased his forward momentum, turned to face the detective, and sat on the floor, resuming his previous position.

"That guy's an asshole, Detective. I'd like to kick the hell out of that little shit," he pouted. "He has no right to search my car... you should know that! I'll kick his prissy little ass!"

"Well, that's not going to happen, Mr. Avion. You won't be kicking any ass," Manny snapped back, avoiding the issue of his car. "If you want to make a big deal out of this, I'll haul you downtown for a few hours. You want to do it that way? I'm more than happy to give you guest accommodations for a while, if that's what you want."

"No," came the meek reply. "I've got things to do today. But they can't look through my car!"

"Why not, Mr. Avion? Is there something in there you don't want us to see?"

The man on the floor sat silent for several seconds. He studied the detective's face carefully. The survey ended with that tight, annoying smile — apparently, his trademark expression.

"No," he answered. "There's nothing in there but junk. But it's *my* junk."

Manny sat back in the chair and studied the man in front of him. He was huge and obviously strong, yet he relied on his wit, not his brawn. He was a thinker, a manipulator. He said it all with his hazy blue eyes, his crazy straight smile, and the dancing motion of his stout fingers when he talked. This guy was always on stage and, today, Bruin and his comrades played the role of audience. Lionell had been right. This guy was sharper than most.

For several moments, neither man spoke. Avion stared down at the shag rug, pulling at one of the loose threads with his stubby fingers. Bruin studied the top of the man's head, watching the slight bobbing motion that never seemed to move his stiff, thick crew cut. Finally, the detective could wait no longer. Avion had won the battle of silence, but the detective still had one surprise waiting for him.

Bruin stood up and reached to his left, grabbing the end table by one leg and dragging it toward him across the uneven rug. He positioned it between his chair and where Avion sat on the floor. The detective pulled a sheet from his inside jacket pocket, unfolded it, and laid it on the table in front of Avion. He carefully teased the wrinkles from its face and aligned it so that his suspect could read the typewritten words at the top of the page.

"Please read the sentences at the top," he said, gesturing toward the page. "Read them carefully."

"Why?" Avion asked, staring at the page. "Why do I have to read this? What is this for?"

"I want you to read it and then copy the words in your own printing, at the bottom of the page where the blank space is. Do you see that?" Bruin asked in a friendly way.

"I don't have a pencil," Avion complained. "I don't having anything to write with."

Bruin produced a black felt-tip pen. He pulled off the plastic cap, affixed it to the end of the pen, and laid it next to the page on the table. Avion stared at the pen with a straight smile, then back at the page in front of him. The lines read:

> I want you to print this cipher
> on the front page of your paper.
> In this cipher is my identity.
> School children make nice tar-
> gets, etc, I think I shall wipe out
> a school bus some morning.

"Okay, Mr. Avion," Bruin said after several minutes. "You've had a chance to read this now, so please print it out for me. I want you to print it, not write it. Okay?"

"Print it," Avion echoed.

"Yes."

"Is this in the warrant?" the big man asked. "Do I have to do this thing?" The words were argumentative, but the tone of his voice was indifferent.

"Yes, you do," came the cold reply. "Either do it here or we will do it at the station. It's your choice."

Avion gave a heavy sigh and picked up the pen with his right hand. He painstakingly copied each letter of each word. To Bruin, the process was too metered, too contrived. When Avion had finished, he laid the pen down next to the page but said nothing.

"Please do it again, Mr. Avion. This time with your left hand."

"I can't!" came the reply. "I'm right-handed, not left."

"Please try it anyway." It was an order. There was no room for discussion.

Avion grumbled something and reluctantly picked up the pen with his left hand. He struggled mightily for several moments, trying to create each letter as carefully as he could. Bruin could see that the result was a mess, with disjointed strokes and uneven alignment. If this man was left-handed or ambidextrous, he was doing a masterful job of covering his tracks.

When Avion had finally finished, the Detective made him copy the words again, this time with his right hand. Then, again, with his left. His right, his left, until the Detective had managed to fill the page with samples. Throughout the process, Avion said nothing. He would sigh, sometimes grumble to himself, but never look directly at Bruin. Still, he did what he was told, and with each try, the handwriting seemed to flow a bit more smoothly, with more purpose.

Finally, they were done. The bottom of the page was filled with samples, as was a second blank sheet that the detective had produced. Bruin retrieved the exemplars, which he carefully folded and put back into his jacket pocket. The pen followed. For a few moments, they sat in silence, not looking at each other. Avion seemed to be drifting away, strangely indifferent. Bruin had to deal with one final issue before he was ready to leave.

"You don't live here, do you Mr. Avion?" he asked in a soothing, friendly tone. "I mean, you have another place up here, don't you? This isn't your primary Santa Rosa residence?"

Avion looked directly at him, for the first time in a half-hour, trying to gauge the importance of the question. Once again, he offered that annoying smile. Or was it a smirk?

"Sometimes yes, sometimes no," he said. "My official address is in San Francisco."

"At your mother's house..." the detective filled in.

"Yes. My mother's house in San Francisco..."

"But you don't live there either, do you?"

"Sometimes yes, sometimes no."

"Where else do you live, Mr. Avion? No one of your intelligence lives like this. You don't live here, but you have a lot going on in the area, don't you? Where do you live, Mr. Avion?"

The man stared away at the far wall, weighing his answer. His eyes drifted closed and his head dropped slightly. Then, the one response that Bruin did not want to hear.

"This interview is over, Detective. I want to call my lawyer."

Manny slid forward from the chair and stood up. The game was over and he knew it. Obviously, Avion knew it too. He had pulled the chain.

"That won't be necessary, Mr. Avion. The interview is over now," Bruin snapped. He brushed past the man on the floor and stepped to the door. Avion jumped up and followed him, close enough to touch the back of the detective's jacket. Manny whipped around and gave Avion a stern push in the chest. Avion looked shocked and stared down at his chest where Bruin's hand had landed.

"That was a pretty gutsy move for a little guy," he said through clenched teeth. "That was pretty gutsy..."

Bruin smiled — a deliberately mean, crusty smile that was meant to mimic Avion's own. Without another word, he stepped around the half-open door into the hallway, leaving Avion standing at the threshold.

"They better not mess with my car!" Avion spat at the inspector's back. "They better leave my car alone." He slammed the door and disappeared into his room.

Somehow, Manny knew that Byron Avion wasn't really worried about Lionell and Millian rummaging through his car. It was all a part of the game — a game that Avion played and everyone else tried to join. He knew Avion understood that such a search could never happen — legally. There was no cause to search the car, and it wasn't covered in the warrant. The best the inspectors could do was to stare through the dirty, smoke-oiled windows at the junk that was strewn all over the seats and floor. That old, white Chevy sedan had more on Avion's personality in one square foot of discarded papers, books, and clothing than anything they had found in his apartment. Too bad they hadn't thought of that. Too bad they hadn't thought about the car. Now, they'd just have to get it the old-fashioned way — without a warrant.

Their plans were made over stale, over-steeped coffee in a rambling, plastic diner near Avion's enigmatic apartment. It was a hangout for the college crowd. The three of them talked, and Sam Lionell finally calmed down. They looked carefully at the handwriting samples and agreed to send them to the SFPD analysts and then on to Sacramento, although Lionell was convinced that there was not a match to be found. Bruin and Lionell bantered about whether or not Avion had faked the handwriting; whether or not he was left-handed or ambidextrous. In the end, they decided that the samples proved nothing, one way or the other. They either didn't match the serial killer's writing or the investigators had simply been outwitted by their suspect. They didn't know. Lionell's worst fears had been realized – the whole search had been a bust.

Finally, they decided to meet that night, very late, and do a number on Avion's car — get a look at the junk inside. Find something. Say nothing to anyone. They discussed it quietly, secretly, and arranged all the details. Mick Millian also agreed to dog Avion as much as possible over the coming months. The guy was up to something. The all knew it — they all could feel it.

But no one ever saw the Chevy again. At least no one who lived to tell about it. When Lionell, Bruin and Millian arrived at Avion's apartment late that night, the car was gone. What troubled Lionell most about the missing sedan was that it matched the description of the vehicle seen speeding away from the Lake Berryessa area on the afternoon of September 27, 1969. Now, he was completely frustrated and ready to go back to the City, ready to think about anything other than the Zodiac.

Bruin and Millian would work hard over the next two years to locate that sedan, but it never reappeared.

Getting to Know You

Mick Millian's word to his partner was good, although it came with a heavy personal price. What started out as a routine surveillance assignment quickly evolved into confusion, frustration and anger. After the June 4 search of Avion's apartment, Millian spent hundreds of hours over the next six months dogging Sam Lionell's suspect. The detective's social life, minimal to begin with, evaporated into a long string of late nights in front of Avion's apartment and countless afternoons trying to ferret out his disordered comings and goings. By the end of that summer, though, Millian had put together a fair amount of information about his man. In the end, it painted a strange, distorted portrait of an individual who either had something to hide, or was just plain crazy.

Early in the summer, Avion split his time between his mother's house in San Francisco and his hovel in Santa Rosa. He was working two part-time jobs: a few hours each week as a stockman in a San Francisco department store and two nights a week as a janitor at the Del Bridge Elementary School near the Santa Rosa Junior College campus. By the end of the summer, he had given up the job in San Francisco and was spending more and more time in Santa Rosa. At the beginning of September, his janitorial job went from two nights a week to four.

Throughout that summer and into the early fall, Millian was careful to stay in the shadows. He spoke to no one except Manny Bruin about Avion's activities. Despite the fact that Millian kept his distance and maintained his patience, he began to get the gnawing feeling that his prey knew something was going on. Avion's movements were too careful, too circumscribed and unpredictable to be routine. After a few months of trailing Avion nearly every day, it dawned on Millian that he was developing far more questions than answers. Yes, he was learning a good deal about his man, but much of it was contradictory, inexplicable, and sometimes downright nonsensical.

By the end of the summer, Millian had learned that his suspect drove at least four different vehicles, excluding the white Chevy sedan that had apparently vanished without a trace. On at least a dozen occasions, Millian watched his prey emerge from his apartment late at night and head for a green Volkswagen that he routinely parked a block away. Avion would stuff his frame into the little car and tear away, leading Millian on a fifteen-minute excursion of Santa Rosa's back streets before he pulled over and took to the sidewalk again. He would walk for a few blocks, then jump into another vehicle, sometimes a van and sometimes an older black sedan, and repeat the entire process, this time using a different route. Time after time, Millian had been left in the dust when Avion changed transportation. Each time, though, Mick would get a little closer, last a little longer on the chase. But Avion simply had too many cars, too many detours, and too many stops for the detective to keep up. In the end, Mick learned two things: his man had at least four vehicles, and he had no idea where Avion was heading once he shook the tail. The frustration brought on by these strange chases pushed Millian into an absolute rage more than once.

And there was more. Avion rarely spent time in his apartment near the college campus. After a few months of dogging him, Millian also discovered that his man was spending less and less time in San Francisco. So where did he go? Avion was a master at disappearing at the most inconvenient times. He would often be gone for two or three days on end between Millian's stints at work. It was obvious to the detective that his man had some other residence — but he had no idea where that was.

In the many months that Millian followed Avion, he never saw the big man alone with another person. When he was on campus or out in public, the suspect never walked with another person and rarely spoke to anyone nearby. He never went grocery shopping, never went to the laundromat around the corner from his apartment, and Millian never saw him stop any of his fleet at a gas station. If he wasn't at work, on the Santa Rosa Junior College campus, or in one of his vehicles, he was hidden away in that tiny sanctum on College Way South.

Occasionally, Millian would catch Avion sitting behind the wheel of his green Volkswagen, apparently watching the world go by. When he was near the campus, Avion would park in front of the administration building, directly across from the broad walkway that led to the heart of the school, and watch the students coming and going. Mick thought he showed a special interest in the hundreds of young co-eds that passed by his post, but he was never close enough to know for sure. Twice in December, Millian caught Avion parked across the street from the Northridge Ice Skating Rink in downtown Santa Rosa, watching the patrons as they came in and out. On those occasions, the big man sat for nearly an hour, completely still behind the wheel, before he tore off to begin his game of car swapping.

During that time, Millian had only been caught once with his pants down. In late August he was at his usual post, watching the apartment on College Way South. It was well after midnight. Mick was exhausted but wanted to wait just a while longer — just in case — so he decided to get some caffeine. Remembering where he, Bruin, and Lionell had first made their plans after the June visit to Avion's apartment, Millian left his car parked across the street and walked to the plastic diner with the stale coffee. He ordered a large one to go and began to walk out the door when he ran right into Byron Avion on his way in. There was no time to duck and cover, so he just kept on going, sliding past the big man just as he entered the restaurant. Avion said nothing; neither did Mick. That was the last time Mick ventured into the restaurant.

During those interminable months, Mick kept Manny up-to-date on Avion. Bruin and Lionell talked a few times each week, mostly about Lionell's investigation and worsening ulcer. Finally, in December, Lionell gave in to the stress of years on the job and was hospitalized with a stomach lining that looked like last month's cottage cheese. It cost him five months on the home front, but he eventually returned to the chase. In the meantime, the Zodiac investigation had taken another turn for the worse and Lionell was having a hell of a time piecing things together. It was Christmas 1971 before Manny finally began to put things together about Byron Avion. He was beginning to think that Lionell might have been right all along.

There was nothing about Byron Avion that was simple or straightforward. Against the uncertain and chaotic background of the Zodiac investigation, he *seemed* like a reasonable suspect — perhaps even a leading one. But that possibility was also far from simple or straightforward. From Sam Lionell's point of view, Avion was definitely a hot item, but also an elusive one. Everything the San Francisco inspector had gathered against him was circumstantial, or worse.

Throughout 1971 and into early 1972, Manny Bruin became increasingly interested in what was going on with Byron Avion, based mostly on Millian's surveillance and Avion's remarkable ability to draw a cloak of secrecy around everything he did. Both Manny and Mick agreed that this guy was up to no good, and probably had some indescribable connection with the Zodiac investigation, but neither man could put a finger on it. Either that, or he was leading them on one of the strangest, most meaningless pursuits that they had ever undertaken. Regardless, it seemed like Avion was doing the real fishing while the two detectives were left to nibble at his bait.

Shortly after Sam Lionell was released from the hospital, he telephoned Bruin to catch up on things. The two talked a good deal about the letters that Zodiac had written to the San Francisco *Chronicle* between the summer of 1969 and early 1971. By this time, Bruin had managed to get photocopies of each of the letters from the SFPD and study them carefully. What Lionell pointed out during their phone call was something that Bruin had wondered about for several weeks. Zodiac's last letter to the *Chronicle* had been written on March 22, 1971. The three detectives had searched Avion's apartment in June — less than three months later. Since then, the Zodiac had inexplicably fallen silent. He had written no letters to the *Chronicle*, or anywhere else. Sam Lionell thought that this was a major point in favor of considering Avion a solid suspect. Bruin agreed, but he wasn't completely convinced. He was looking for something more, something certain.

The question of timing proved to be an interesting and unexpected turn of events in the Zodiac investigation. The killer had written letters in July, August, October, and November of 1969 to three different newspapers, although he clearly favored the *Chronicle*. In December of that year he wrote to San Francisco attorney Melvin Belli. In 1970, he wrote to the *Chronicle* in April, June, July, and October. He then waited until March 1971, when he wrote to both the Los Angeles *Times* and the *Chronicle*. It certainly looked as if his pattern of writing would continue into the remainder of 1971 as it had in 1970. But then, he suddenly stopped, and didn't pen another letter for the rest of the year.

There was nothing in Zodiac's last letters that indicated he intended to stop using the media as his personal forum. To the contrary, he wrote as if he wanted to keep up the pressure, and was enjoying the game. So, why did he suddenly stop? Sam Lionell thought it was because Zodiac knew that his pursuers were too close. From Bruin's perspective, there were any number of other possibilities that also fit the facts. The fugitive could have died, been jailed for some other crime, left the area, or simply decided to stop writing.

Mick Millian had discovered a number of other quirks in Avion's behavior that moved him closer to the top of the Zodiac list. He had an obvious penchant for white nylon rope, the kind used for backyard clotheslines. Avion often used it to tie the cuffs of his pants to his boots. On several occasions, Millian had seen him carrying cardboard boxes from his car to his apartment and back. These boxes were invariably tied with the same kind of nylon rope. Mick had seen loops of this rope strewn around the seats and floorboards of three of Avion's vehicles. Zodiac had used this same kind of rope to tie his Lake Berryessa victims before stabbing them. Napa County authorities had recovered strands of that rope, and both Bruin and Millian had had the chance to examine them. Obviously, Avion was not the only person north of San Francisco to carry and use nylon clothesline rope, but it did make an interesting point.

There were other things. The handwriting samples that Bruin had gathered in June 1971 and turned over to Sam Lionell were later analyzed at the State Crime Division in Sacramento. Although they did not match the known handwriting of the wanted serial killer, experts agreed that Avion's exemplars were misleading. They decided that the man who penned the samples had deliberately tried to cover up his own handwriting style. They were also convinced that the Avion samples were written by a man who was ambidextrous. Zodiac was thought to be ambidextrous.

Millian had come up with a healthy list of points that *could* connect Avion with the Zodiac investigation. These included times, locations, vehicles, witness statements, and information provided by tipsters. Avion lived in San Francisco — Zodiac mailed his letters from there. Avion wore a particular style of work boot that closely matched footprint impressions at two of Zodiac's crime scenes. He was a reasonable, though not close, match to eyewitness descriptions of the killer. On and on. The problem was that, as one went farther down the list, each point seemed to lose something. The connections became looser and more vague. There was nothing that could directly tie Avion to the unsolved murders, and there was no hope of taking any action against him. In the end, the three investigators agreed that this guy was definitely someone worth watching, but they disagreed on the reasons. All they really shared was that certain sense — that sixth sense — that all good investigators carry in their back pockets.

By the first days of 1971, Byron Avion had become a bigger-than-life problem for everyone involved. Lionell was physically exhausted and seriously ill, certainly not ready to resume the hunt anytime soon. But he desperately wanted to find some closure to the case. Millian had gone from interested to frustrated to enraged at Avion's antics and his uncanny ability to stay just beyond reach. Manny had his hands full with trying to keep Mick in reasonable waters and still manage their other cases. But he found himself drawn ever deeper into the Zodiac investigation and Avion's apparent connection to it. All three needed a break from the case, and they needed it soon. Unfortunately, they would get it in all the wrong ways.

In the winter of 1972, Bruin and Millian would be torn away from their interest in the Zodiac investigation, at least for a time. Their fascination with Byron Avion, however, would turn into an obsession that would haunt them both for decades.

Vanishings

Everyone loves a hometown hero. In the winter of 1968, Peggy Fleming won the Olympic gold medal for women's figure skating in an electrifying performance seen on television sets across America. Peggy was born in San Jose, about 100 miles south of Santa Rosa, which made her nearly a hometowner by local standards. When she took the gold, little girls all over Northern California took to ice skating in droves. Dreams of becoming an Olympic skater overtook countless thousands of youngsters in the 1960s, even in such far-flung and forgotten outposts as Santa Rosa, where ice-skating once seemed to be more a foreign pastime than a sport.

Four years later, in 1972, the Olympic Games were held in Sapporo, Japan, just a hop across the pond from the Northern California coast for Santa Rosans with winter sports on their mind. This despite the fact that Santa Rosa sees snow perhaps once every 20 years. Many of those same young girls who had been so enraptured with Peggy Fleming four years earlier once again traded in their summer shorts for mittens, and their springboard belly flops for a day of practicing school figures at the local ice rink. Two of these local youngsters were Mary Spooner and Elaine Calley.

Mary and Elaine were both twelve years old, both seventh graders at the Del Bridge Elementary School, and the best of friends. They were smallish, bright, talkative girls, who even looked alike with their faded blonde hair and a smattering of freckles across their noses. The Spooner and Calley families had settled on the same block in East Santa Rosa, close to the junior college, when the girls were only toddlers. It was a neighborhood overflowing with young families, kids of all ages, and neatly kept houses with broad, deep backyards. Most of the residents were first-time homeowners, who had settled in the area because of the family-oriented environment and the relatively low cost of housing.

John Spooner owned a busy, promising hardware franchise on the outskirts of downtown, while Bill Calley worked as a senior clerk in the Sonoma County court system. Julie Spooner and Cathy Calley were primarily housewives and mothers, although Cathy earned some extra money as a part-time travel agent. The Spooners had a second, younger daughter, Yvette, who was in the fourth grade. Elaine Calley was an only child and the complete focus of her parent's love and attention.

Since before the first grade, the two girls had been inseparable. The Spooner and Calley families were also close, often spending evenings playing cards and chatting, while the girls entertained themselves in one or the other's bedroom. On summer weekends, John and Bill would often go fishing together at their favorite hideaway along the Russian River, about an hour's drive west. In the winter, they would shoot pool at the nearby bowling alley or hang out at the local pub to watch Monday Night Football and share some beer.

When they were eight years old, Mary and Elaine watched in awe as Peggy Fleming captured the gold. That day, in front of Mary's television set, they knew that they had both found their role model and their future. They agreed that they each wanted to grow up to be just like Peggy — beautiful, graceful, and famous. Within a few days of the Olympics' closing ceremonies, both girls had convinced their parents to buy them ice skates and shuttle them back and forth to the Northridge Ice Skating Rink, the only ice rink in town. The Spooners and Calleys were happy with their daughters' choice of activity. It seemed fitting for the two girls and a healthy, safe way to spend the winter months indoors. Besides, who wouldn't want their daughter to grow up to be like Peggy Fleming?

For the next four years, Mary and Elaine kept up their passion for ice skating, although they were inevitably drawn to other interests during the extended, warm summers. By seventh grade, the girls were looking forward to the precious high school years that lay just ahead. They had begun to share their newly blossoming interest in boys — a topic that seemed to occupy more and more of their discussions since the beginning of the school year. It was an exciting, wonderful time to be twelve-going-on-thirteen in a town flush with children their age and made free by the safety of their family ties and familiar community. That is, until the end of February 1972.

On the afternoon of Richard Nixon's last day of his momentous trip to China, Mary and Elaine grabbed their ice skates and asked Cathy Calley for a ride to the Northridge rink. They could have walked there — it was only ten blocks — but it was quicker to drive and Elaine's Mom always felt better about it. The girls planned to spin around the ice for an hour or so, then return to their respective homes for the family dinner that was a tradition with both the Spooners and the Calleys. As was often the case, Mary and Elaine were dressed similarly, in faded blue jeans and white blouses. Mary wore a pink jacket with a hood and Elaine a brown, pullover sweater. Both had their blonde hair pulled back into ponytails and each was wearing a set of delicate gold loops in their ears. The earrings were identical and had been given to the girls by John Spooner the previous Christmas.

When Mrs. Calley pulled her Jeep to a stop in front of the ice skating rink, the girls assured her that they would call for a ride back in an hour or so, in plenty of time for dinner. With that, Mary and Elaine hopped excitedly out of the car and disappeared into the rambling, brightly painted corner building.

Louise Gensen, the owner of the Northridge rink and a long-time resident of Sonoma County, knew both girls well and liked them enormously. They were regular customers, lively, polite, chatty, and naturally charming. Besides that, they had a love of ice-skating that naturally pulled at Louise's heart. A woman of forty, she had once tried out for the U. S. Juniors team but was bumped at the last moment and was never able to regain her form. Her hopes of a career on the ice were quickly overcome with the realities of economic survival in a small town. However, her love of the sport never died. She was eventually able to scrape together enough money and outside financing to open her own rink. Northridge never did well economically, but it survived, thanks mostly to regulars like Mary Spooner and Elaine Calley.

Gensen saw the two girls arrive that afternoon, at about four o'clock, and spoke with them for a few moments while they strapped on their skates. Mary and Elaine were especially excited that afternoon. A seventh grade winter dance had been scheduled for the following Saturday at their school and the two were deep in the process of rating the boys who were likely to attend. Mary and Elaine had already decided to go together so they could make on-site, in-depth comparisons of their male classmates. It was their first dance, and their expectations were high.

The girls took to the mostly empty ice, practiced some rudimentary school figures, and chatted with a few skating friends for about an hour. Just after five o'clock, they sat down on a wooden bench by the side of the rink and removed their skates. Neither Mary nor Elaine had remembered to bring change for the public telephone near the front of the building, so Mary decided to ask Louise if she could use the office phone. While dialing, Mary again told Louise how excited she was about the dance. Cathy Spooner answered and told her daughter that she would be in front of the skating rink in 15 minutes. A few minutes after the call, Louise saw the girls leave by the front door, carrying their skates in their hands.

Paul Buchette, a lifelong resident of the Santa Rosa area and a retired elementary schoolteacher, owned and operated the corner grocery store directly across the street from the Northridge Ice Skating Rink. Like Louise Gensen, Buchette knew and liked Mary and Elaine. They would often cross the street to his store after a skating session in search of a cold drink or Elaine's favorite snack, Granny Goose BBQ potato chips. The stout, sixty-something, white-bearded owner would often chat with the girls about their skating and schoolwork, usually punctuating his conversation with enhanced memories of what Mary and Elaine thought were the "dark ages" of Sonoma County. Over the four years that Buchette had known the girls, he had become very attached to them. Everyone had.

Working his struggling 1940s cash register at the front window of the cluttered store that afternoon, Buchette noticed Mary and Elaine standing in front of the skating rink just after five o'clock. Through his scratched bifocals, the old man thought that they were looking in his direction, so Buchette raised a burly hand and waved at them from behind the glass. Rather than waving back as he had expected, the girls turned in unison, as if they had heard something, and stared northward, away from the front door to the skating rink and up the street. Then they began to walk together, slowly, in the same direction. For a moment, Paul took his eyes away from the girls as a customer came into his store. He greeted the young woman with a nod, and then turned again to follow the progress of his two young friends. To his surprise, they were nowhere in sight.

At the time, Buchette assumed that the girls had gotten into one of their mother's cars, although he hadn't seen it happen. That had been a long-standing habit with Mary and Elaine, and it made Paul feel better about seeing them alone on the busy street. That afternoon, he made the usual assumption and didn't give it another thought. He hadn't paid much attention to the battered green Volkswagen that had been parked across the street and up the block for about an hour. That was not the kind of thing one usually worried about in Santa Rosa.

By 5:30, Cathy Calley was double-parked, waiting in her Jeep outside the skating rink, but the girls were nowhere in sight. Frustrated and anxious to get home to begin dinner, she moved her vehicle up the block, locked it, and went into the building. Louise Gensen, who was working in the windowless office at the front of the skating rink, saw her enter and came out to say hello. When Mrs. Calley learned that the girls had left the rink a half-hour earlier, her heart dropped. Mary and Elaine had never done this kind of thing before. If they said they would be somewhere, then that's where they would be. There were simply no exceptions. Cathy's frustration quickly turned to fear.

Cathy called the Spooner home from Louise Gensen's phone and learned that neither of the girls had shown up. She spoke to Julie Spooner, and the two mothers decided to make separate searches of the routes that their daughters might have taken if they had decided to walk home. They would meet at Cathy's house in a half-hour and decide what to do if they hadn't found the girls.

The impromptu search for Mary and Elaine proved fruitless. After the two mothers met at Cathy's house, they canvassed the neighborhood, called all their daughters' friends, and broke the news to their husbands as they each returned home from work. By eight o'clock that night, the Spooners and Calleys agreed that they had done everything that they could think of. It was time to call for help.

In 1970s Sonoma County, missing children cases were still unusual events, especially if the kids were young, predictable, stable, and well-known in the community, like Mary Spooner and Elaine Calley. The families first contacted the Santa Rosa Police Department and then the Sonoma County Sheriff's Office. Both agencies responded immediately and sent an officer to the distraught parents, who had set themselves up in the Calley home to coordinate their efforts and provide mutual support. Officers from both the SRPD and the SCSO took detailed incident reports, descriptions and family photographs of the girls, and offered as much encouragement as they could. They also arranged to have Mary and Elaine's physical descriptions broadcast to personnel in the field. If the kids were not found by the next afternoon, missing persons reports would be filed and sent to all local jurisdictions, and both agencies would open a coordinated investigation. In the meantime, the SRPD would interview anyone in the area of the Northridge Ice Skating Rink, just in case someone had seen something that could be of help.

That first night was a horrific torture for the Spooner and Calley families, but it would prove to be just the beginning. The two agencies working the missing persons case had no leads whatsoever and were never able to generate much information about the girls' disappearance. Louise Gensen had only seen Mary and Elaine leave the rink that afternoon. She had no idea what had happened after that. Paul Buchette had seen the girls; he had waved at them. He saw them walking up the street. But he didn't recall anything suspicious. They hadn't been talking to anyone outside the skating rink. No, nothing else that he could remember. The old man was clearly concerned and repeatedly offered his help, but he really had nothing of importance for the investigation.

Three days after the girls disappeared, a force of nearly 100 volunteers from the Santa Rosa area began searching for Mary and Elaine. Among those who helped organize this unprecedented effort was Mick Millian, one of Bill Calley's closest friends. Mick and Bill had been raised together in the rural Russian River area, west of Santa Rosa, and had remained good friends. Bill had called Mick late on the night that his daughter disappeared, telling him what had happened and asking what else he could do to get her back. Millian suggested the volunteer effort and arranged to have the Santa Rosa *Journal* cover the disappearance, publish the girls' photographs, and announce his intention to assemble volunteers. Over the next few days, he organized the volunteers as they came forward, arranged to coordinate efforts with the SRPD and the SCSO, and kept the families and press up-to-date. Bill Calley would later tell a reporter from the Santa Rosa *Journal* that Mick Millian had been the single most important source of support for the two families throughout their sickening ordeal.

Within a week of the girls' disappearance, it became obvious to the law enforcement community that the worst outcome was possible — even likely — although publicly they remained upbeat and optimistic. The families had received no ransom demands, searches had provided no clues, and no witness information was forthcoming. Although the Calleys and Spooners kept their hopes alive, and the volunteers under Mick Millian's supervision continued to search, the days turned into weeks without any reason for optimism. It would be some ten months before the mystery was finally solved.

During the months following Mary and Elaine's disappearance, Millian stayed very close to the investigation and tried to support the members of both families as much as he could, especially Bill Calley and his wife. Mick's old friend had been pushed to the very edge of his endurance. Usually controlled, reliable, and steadfast, Bill had become frequently enraged and depressed, and was unable to work for more than two months. Millian spent dozens of nights with Bill, working over the possibilities, inventing scenarios, and trying to remain positive in the fading hope of finding the girls alive. Gently, almost imperceptibly, Mick tried to bring Bill to the realization that Elaine and her best friend might never be found alive or, worse, might never be found at all. It was the way these tragedies often played out.

At first, Bill was furious with Millian, and refused to entertain that kind of a possibility. Later, though, he began to accept the idea. Gradually, Mick turned Bill toward considering *all* the options, working toward resolving the mystery, but preparing himself, his family, and the Spooners for the worst news that they could imagine. By the early summer, Bill Calley had managed to pull himself together sufficiently to return to work. He spent his free days assembling and reassembling the facts of the case, interviewing folks in the neighborhood of the skating rink, and keeping a daily journal to ease his suffering.

Bill Calley's desperate work finally paid off in early July during a discussion with Paul Buchette. By this time, Paul and Bill had become more than acquaintances. Calley had interviewed the aging storekeeper several times, always going over the same infertile ground, searching for something that both men had overlooked. Paul had given the distressed father a good deal of sympathy and had answered all his questions as well as he could. Yes, he knew the girls and liked them very much. No, he hadn't seen anything out of the ordinary. It seemed like just another one of their trips to the skating rink. Well, maybe there was one thing. There was that little green bug, that Volkswagen, which was parked across the street that day. That was a bit strange, the old man supposed. He hadn't noticed it in the neighborhood before.

Calley pressed the shopkeeper about the Volkswagen. What did it look like? Who was driving it? Did the girls talk to the driver? Did you get a license number? Why didn't you tell the SRPD or the Sheriff's officers?

Bill and Paul talked for the best part of an hour about that car. The old man hadn't considered it to be important. In fact, he hadn't even recalled the car until something Bill said triggered his memory. No, he didn't know who was driving it. The guy was in the shadows, but he seemed like a large man. He just sat behind the wheel for an hour or so. No, he never saw the girls go near the car. They just walked up the street, toward where it was parked. No, he couldn't recall anything else. Sorry.

Bill was the first to admit that it wasn't much, but at least it was something new and it had a definite ring of familiarity. He decided to call Mick that afternoon, to share the news and find out what to do next. That call would permanently focus Millian's attention on Byron Avion — the man Bruin had begun calling "Suspect Zero" in recognition of his uncanny ability to be both a tantalizing suspect and no suspect at all. For Millian, this enigmatic, frustrating man would soon become much more than just an interesting suspect. He would become an obsession.

April 1972
Cathy Alverson

April was a chameleon month that year, as it often is in Northern California. One day it was bright and pleasant, with temperatures in the low 70s and just the hint of a breeze from the Pacific Ocean, which lies about an hour's drive to the west. The next day it would be rainy, blustery, and unusually cold. Still, there were more good days than bad, and summer seemed to be lurking somewhere nearby, waiting for its final cue to sweep onstage.

The onset of summer worried Manny Bruin, although he was careful to keep it to himself. It was a vague sort of thing, anyway — a kind of apprehension that always seemed to overtake him in the spring. Perhaps it was just that Sonoma County was so often overrun with new faces by the fullness of summer, and that meant more case files and much more work than he had time to handle.

Perhaps it was just something about *this* particular spring, this particular summer. He wasn't sure.

This morning, Bruin stood next to Mick Millian in the thin sunshine on a graveled turnout at the edge of Old Miner's Forge Road, three miles east of downtown Santa Rosa. Below the two men was an unnamed, narrow, sixty-foot-deep culvert, now populated with a cadre of uniformed SCSO officers, SRPD personnel, a forensic technician from the SCCID, and the Assistant Medical Examiner for the County, Cynthia Turgell. The heart of the group was hovering around the nude body of a young woman, who lay in the black shadows where the edge of the culvert met the raised roadway.

The impression made on passing motorists that morning must have been of an impromptu police convention. Making their appearance were several fast, brown sedans for the SCSO folks, a gaggle of blue and white cruisers for the SRPD officers, a black two-door for the forensics technician, and a pristine white van for the ME contingent. They were lined up along the gravelly shoulder, looking like a marooned caravan.

Standing at the north lip of the culvert was Howard Vorhies, the Sonoma County Medical Examiner. At 68, he looked much older than his years and exceptionally tired, with a permanent bend in his posture that had been brought on by more than twenty years hovering over bodies at crimes scenes and autopsies. By 1972, Vorhies was more than ready to retire, more than ready to turn over the reins to his bright, energetic assistant. In recent months, he had also become gruff, unruly, and unusually sullen. Still, he was a favorite with the law enforcement community in Sonoma County, who had come to rely on his ability to ferret out even the most tangled wrongful-death cases.

Old Miner's Forge Road is a twisting, ill-mannered, mostly ignored country lane that connects with Highway 101 at two points: the first is two miles north of downtown Santa Rosa, the other a mile south of town, leading toward Petaluma. It's a rural, eucalyptus-lined bypass for locals who dislike the chaos of the freeway or those few who live in the rolling, brush-covered hills beyond the overly populated East Side. In 1972, it was a road that saw very little traffic, except for area residents who managed to eke out a living from the land. The culvert, which ran for quite a stretch along the far side of the road, was a good place to pull to the shoulder, dump a body, and be gone in a matter of seconds without fear of interruption. It was an exceptionally quiet, isolated, and dark place.

Bruin shuffled his feet in the dusty gravel and stared off into the hills. The sparse, undulating brush and wild grasses were exceptionally green this time of year, unlike most months when they looked more like interminable patches of faded yellow and brown carpet. The hills directly above the culvert were punctuated by lonely clusters of black-and-white Holsteins, meandering lazily in the cool morning, indifferent to the unusual sound of voices from the road below.

From where Manny stood, there was only one home to be seen in the immediate area. It was a rambling, wooden, dirty white farmhouse that belonged to Sarge Perkins — a local dairyman, now in his late 70s — and his family of six. The patriarchal house sat astride a single-lane dirt road, nearly a mile into the hills. Not a likely place to find a witness. Bruin's instincts told him that whoever dumped this body had chosen this site with care.

Even more interesting was *how* the victim wound up in the culvert. Her killer, or whoever had dumped her there, would have had to throw the body over a four-foot-high guardrail in order to get it to the bottom of the depression. Either that, or he had to walk clear over to the north edge of the depression and carry her down the steep embankment to the bottom. Whoever had thrown or put the body down there was not a lightweight.

"Who do you think she is?" Millian whispered, interrupting Bruin's machinations. "She looks pretty young from up here."

Manny shook his head, dropping his gaze from the home nestled in the hills to the comings and goings of the officers below. They were scrambling along the steep faces of the culvert, working their way carefully through the undergrowth to look for evidence. Uneven streams of broad yellow tape had already appeared around the perimeter and were rustling noisily in the morning breeze. One of the SCSO officers was taking photographs of the body and the surrounding ground. Another was poking around the area a bit to the north, carefully pulling away clumps of loose brush to look underneath.

"Who's missing, Mick? I mean, do we have anything fresh going on? Anyone gone missing in the last few days? Does the woman who found the body have anything to say?"

Millian shook his head. No, she had nothing to add. Just a stroke of luck. She had pulled off the road with her carsick child. She just happened to look around.

He rustled through a wad of stapled papers — copies of recent incident reports from the SCSO and the SRPD about missing persons. As he pushed his way past each page, he let out a soft, humming sound – low for no possibility, a bit higher for something mildly interesting. After two or three minutes, he was finished.

"Well, Manny, I guess there are a few possibilities, but nothing snaps right out at me. A couple of SRJC students went missing, two single females under twenty-five disappeared on the same day, two more in their thirties two weeks apart, and one in her forties about ten days ago. All in the last three months. Maybe one of them — maybe not. I don't know..."

Bruin said nothing. He sucked in a large breath of morning air and watched Cynthia Turgell work her way up the north side of the culvert toward the far end of the turnout. She was carrying the red plastic tackle box that had become her trademark, along with several brown paper sacks containing forensic evidence. The redhead scurried up the slippery clay face with remarkable ease and strode quickly to her boss, Dr. Vorhies. They stood close together and spoke for a few moments. Bruin noticed that Turgell was moving her arms in an animated way, gesturing back and forth from the road to the culvert and making sweeping motions as if she was throwing something down the embankment. At one point, she reached into one of the brown paper sacks and withdrew a plastic baggy that contained something long and white. From where Manny stood, it looked like a piece of rope.

When Turgell and Vorhies had finished their conversation, the elderly doctor turned abruptly and headed directly for his yellow station wagon, which was parked at the far end of the turnout. He slid behind the wheel, fired it up and tore off down the road, apparently heading for town. Manny tried to yell and wave at the departing vehicle, to get Vorhies' attention and demand an explanation, but he was already gone.

"Christ!" Bruin spat. "What the hell was *that* all about? He's supposed to talk to us!"

Mick nudged Bruin's arm with his own and nodded toward the culvert. Cynthia Turgell was moving quickly in their direction, a broad smile on her face.

"Hi, Manny," she said, breathing heavily from her excursion. "I'm sorry, but Dr. Vorhies had to go. He isn't feeling too well, you know. Anyway, he wanted me to handle this case and bring you up to date on what we've found so far. Okay?"

Bruin nodded rapidly. That was fine with him. He liked working with Turgell. Howard was getting to be too grouchy anyway.

"Sure, yeah, that's fine, Cindy. Doc looked pretty tired anyway. Not feeling well?"

"Yeah, not so well," she answered solemnly. "Stomach, heart, and mostly just worn down, I guess. He's a fine man though. Really knows his stuff. He's just been at it a very long time, you know."

Bruin and Millian offered grunts of agreement. Vorhies was a good friend, and they were more than willing to cut him some slack. After all, nobody could take this stuff forever.

"So, what's going on here, Cindy. What do you have?" Bruin asked.

Turgell set her tackle box down and tried to shake some of the thick clay from the sides of her boot. She carefully propped the brown paper bags against the box, freeing both hands. It was her habitual preamble to a lively story. Millian cracked a smile. He loved the way she pieced this stuff together. He loved those stories.

"A young, white, female," she began. "I'd say no more than her early twenties. She's been down there for a few weeks, I'd guess, but mostly protected from predators and insects by the location and the cold climate at the bottom of the culvert. She's nude, no personal effects, no clothing, no jewelry on her person, and no articles near the crime scene, except for this."

Turgell reached into the largest of the paper sacks and pulled out an oversized plastic baggy with a green evidence tag dangling from the top. It held a three-foot-long piece of white nylon rope, like the kind used in backyard clotheslines. She held the bag up to eye level, turned it around a few times, and then passed it on to Bruin before she continued.

"I think she was strangled with that," Turgell announced. "There's definite evidence of strangulation on the remains and it's consistent with that kind of rope, at least at first glance. I think that she was murdered somewhere else then dumped here, Manny. Probably thrown from the edge of the road near that guardrail." The doctor turned and pointed at the spot where Howard Vorhies had stood moments earlier.

"Thrown?" Bruin asked.

"I'd say so, Manny, judging from the position of the body."

"Has anyone examined the area over there for tire tracks?" Bruin grumbled. He was worried about all the foot traffic that had taken the same route to the culvert.

"Yeah, the SCSO guys did it before you got here. Nothing."

"So, no personal effects, no ID or anything like that? Nothing around the body?"

"No. Nope. None," she answered.

"What kind of condition is she in?" Bruin asked. "I mean, we need to get her ID'ed. Can we do that? Do we have enough to do that easily?"

The Doctor smiled and bounced her head up and down. She reached into a second paper sack and pulled out another, much smaller baggy. It contained white fingerprint cards with a fresh set of prints on them.

"Paul from Forensics was able to lift these." She pushed the baggy toward Manny. "We have full prints, except for one finger, and full photos of her face. The body was in remarkably good shape, considering."

"What color was her hair? Her eyes?" Millian mumbled, leafing through the incident reports. "Any identifying characteristics?"

"Let's see... She had red hair, a little darker than mine and longer. She had a flower — a rose — tattooed across the top of her left shoulder. She had a crescent-shaped mole on the top of her left wrist. Let's see..."

"Oh, Christ!" Mick interrupted. He ripped one of the pages from the stapled stack and showed it to Turgell.

"Look at the bottom there," he demanded. "Look at the photo! Look at the description! Is that her?"

Turgell took the incident report, reached into the side pocket of her black jacket, and slipped on a pair of rimless glasses that aged her by ten years. She studied the document, reading it from top to bottom, resisting Millian's order to go directly to the photograph. When she finally reached the bottom of the page, she studied the small black-and-white photo very carefully, then went back to reread the physical description.

"Yeah, Mick, I think so. I think this is her. Catherine Alverson..."

Millian yanked the report away from Turgell and pushed it at Bruin.

"Listen, Manny, she went missing last month. Last seen hitchhiking along the freeway going south, on Highway 101. It was on a Saturday afternoon, last month," he repeated. "I'm sure this is her, right?"

Manny was predictably more reserved. He took a few moments to scan the incident report, and then turned to face his friend. "Yeah, well, it looks good, Mick, but we need to be sure. Cindy, when can you get to this one? Can you do it today?"

"Sure, Manny, I can do it today. We can get her right down to the shop and pull what you need for a positive ID in a couple of hours. A certain cause of death might take a bit longer, but we can do it today."

"Good, good..." he muttered. "I think Mick's right, but I want to make sure. We'll meet you back there later today. In the meantime, we'll go back to SCCID and get the files on this one. Cathy Alverson..."

Turgell nodded, picked up her tackle box and bags, and headed back to the ridge of the culvert to supervise the removal of the body. Millian and Bruin piled back into their sedan and worked their way through town to the SCCID office. They had some cross checking to do and a case file to pull. They had a homicide case to work.

Raised in the hamlet of Guerneville, an overlooked riverside settlement about a forty-minute drive west of Santa Rosa, Catherine Alverson was much more than another cute coed. She was an intelligent, beautiful young woman with rich, auburn hair and penetrating brown, almost black, eyes. She was a natural student, inquisitive and pleasantly serious for her age. Cathy had lived in the town of 1,500 for her entire life, graduating from the Upper Russian River High School in 1970. Her parents, who owned a seasonal restaurant, struggled financially but still managed to give their daughter a sense of herself, her future, and a compassion for others. She was as good as daughters get.

After her high school graduation, Cathy decided to attend Santa Rosa Junior College, primarily because it was all that she could afford. Her father had managed to help Cathy land a job as a waitress at a friend's restaurant in Petaluma, a few miles south of the JC. This would be enough to pay her mostly-subsidized tuition, a modest rent, and scrape out the basic necessities. By the end of summer in 1970, Cathy had made all her plans and was ready to move to a low-budget apartment within walking distance of the SRJC campus. Her new address was 38660 College Way South, one block south and across the street from Byron Avion's residence in 1972.

In the fall of 1970, Cathy enrolled in her first classes, determined to work toward a degree in veterinary medicine at a four-year college. She had no automobile, so the freshman relied on her bicycle or the Sonoma County transit system. The transit system proved to be an unreliable way to travel, and her bike had long ago seen its best years. By 1971, Cathy had taken to the habit of hitchhiking south on Highway 101 to get to her job and bumming a ride back home from one of the other waitresses who lived in the Santa Rosa area.

Cathy's schedule was relentless and predictable, with classes taking up the morning and early afternoon hours, then off to the restaurant for a six-hour shift, six days a week, then back to the studio apartment to study. A few hours sleep and the nineteen-year-old was at it all over again. This routine went unchanged until she disappeared in March 1972.

On weekends, Cathy would telephone her parents. It was always on a Sunday morning. Always. From time to time, mostly in the off-season, her parents would sneak away from the restaurant and drive into Santa Rosa to spend a few hours with their only child. They would always do this on a Saturday morning, arriving early and leaving before it was time for Cathy to go to work.

Cathy Alverson had a boyfriend back in Guerneville, Freddie Revinque, but it had never been a serious, life-altering arrangement. After she left the area, the two kept in touch for a time, but the relationship eventually cooled. Cathy's closest friends were now at her new school, along with a few other coeds that she had met in the apartment complex where she lived. Nothing serious came along in the way of young men. She never really had the time to get involved with them. Cathy had set herself on a determined course toward a life that was more secure than her parents'.

During the same week in March that author Clifford Irving admitted that his interviews and biography of Howard Hughes were nothing but hoaxes, Cathy Alverson vanished. It was on a Saturday afternoon, just after two o'clock. That morning, Cathy had spent a few hours with her parents. They had breakfast at Russo's Restaurant on the West Side, and then strolled through a nearby park before dropping Cathy off at her apartment. The Alversons headed home to the Russian River, and Cathy changed into her work clothes. At two o'clock, she left her apartment and met a friend on the street outside. They chatted for a moment, then Cathy said she was on her way to Petaluma to work and had to get moving. Cathy's friend saw her walk briskly away, heading in the direction of Highway 101. Her intention was to hitchhike south, as she had done many times before.

Alverson never made it to Petaluma. Her employer became concerned around five o'clock and tried to call Cathy's apartment. There was no answer. When no one heard from her by Monday, including several classmates, the SRPD was called and a missing person's report filed. However, since Cathy was 19 years old and living on her own, the SRPD gave the case a low priority. To them, it seemed like one more of a growing number of voluntary disappearances. Understandably, to Cathy's parents, this conclusion was unacceptable. They tried everything they could to get the SRPD and the SCSO involved in their daughter's disappearance. Both agencies were cooperative, polite, and patient, but neither gave the case any kind of priority. It just fell too far down on the food chain in an environment where resources were always scarce. Unlike the disappearance of Mary Spooner and Elaine Calley a month earlier, Alverson's case received no media coverage until her body was discovered a month later. By then, it was major news.

April 1972
Kim Kantell

Less than a week after Cathy Alverson's remains were discovered, another Santa Rosa Junior College co-ed, Kim Kantell, disappeared while hitchhiking north on Highway 101. She was a year older than Cathy, but still a freshman at the JC. Physically, the two women were hauntingly similar. Each had longish auburn hair, dark eyes, a slight frame and trim build. It's possible that Kim and Cathy knew each other, as they were often on the SFJC campus on the same days and at the same times.

Kim Kantell lived with her older sister on the outskirts of Santa Rosa, just north of the city line in a rural area spotted with cheap rentals that had once been budget vacation hideaways. The Kantell sisters had moved here together from Eureka, California, eighteen months earlier in search of adventure in San Francisco. However, like so many other youngsters just starting out, they quickly learned that the inflated cost of living in the City made that dream financially impossible. They settled on the Santa Rosa area, where Kim Kantell enrolled in general education classes at SRJC. Kim also worked part-time in the afternoons at a dry cleaning business three blocks from campus.

Kim Kantell's class schedule was a rather relaxed one that started at mid-morning and finished by the early afternoon. After classes, she would go directly to the dry cleaning business, work until six o'clock or a bit later, and then head home. Her sister's routine was more demanding — she had a morning shift as a checker at a large grocery store in the downtown area. That shift was often extended into the evening; it wasn't unusual for Sandy to put in a twelve-hour day. The result of these different schedules was that Sandy invariably left the house early in the morning to drive to work in the old Ford station wagon that the sisters shared. That left Kim to take the transit system or hitchhike the six miles south to the SRJC campus and then back home again in the evening after work. Like Cathy Alverson, she preferred hitchhiking.

Kim vanished on a Friday, probably around ten in the morning. She was last seen by a Sonoma County work crew as she was hitchhiking south on Highway 101. The six men in the battered orange van couldn't help but notice the pretty young woman standing on the shoulder of the road with her thumb in the air. One of the workmen gave a loud wolf-whistle out the open window — the ensuing ruckus inside the van made the sighting memorable. She never made it to her first class at the JC.

Like Cathy Alverson, Kim Kantell's disappearance barely rippled the media waters in the Santa Rosa area, although it eventually became a hot topic on the SRJC campus. A missing person's report was filed, statements were taken, and a cursory investigation was started. However, there was no reason to look very deeply into the matter, at least from the perspective of the SRPD and the SCSO. There was certainly no evidence of foul play and, like Cathy Alverson, Kim had no known enemies — no one who would want to harm her. Within a few months of her sister's disappearance, the incident was forgotten, and Sandy

Kantell moved back to her family home in Eureka. She never returned to Sonoma County.

Seven years later, the remains of a young woman were found in a shallow grave east of Santa Rosa, near where the bodies of Mary Spooner and Elaine Calley had been dumped. Cynthia Turgell did the work-up on the victim, along with two forensic technicians from the SCCID and an anthropologist. The woman's hands and feet had been bound with white nylon rope. Turgell determined that she might have been strangled to death, maybe even with the same kind of rope, although it was impossible to come to a definite conclusion because of the condition of the remains. A forensic odontologist was eventually called in to examine the teeth of the victim in the hope of making a positive identification. Some similarities were found between the remains and Kim Kantell's scant dental charts. However, once again, it was impossible to come to a final conclusion. To this day, those remains have never been positively identified.

Both Manny Bruin and Mick Millian would later come to believe that the remains discovered in 1979 were those of Kim Kantell. Neither detective was ever able to prove it, but Millian was convinced years earlier that Kim had been abducted and murdered by the same man who had claimed Cathy Alverson.

May 1972
Connections

"We have nothing here, *nada...*" Bruin complained. He slapped the Alverson folder closed and slid it across his desk in Millian's direction. It teetered on the edge for a moment before falling into his lap.

"All we have is one Sonoma County bus driver who *may* have seen her hitchhiking south. Then again, he isn't all that sure, is he? Okay, so we have basically nothing on Alverson. She was strangled, probably that same day, probably with the nylon rope that Turgell found, but we have no suspect. Hell, we aren't even close to connecting a motive to this thing. No one had a reason to kill her. It was a random crime, Mick. Everyone loved this kid..."

"Well, Manny, we've got a *little* more than that, I think," Millian interrupted. "We've got a *little* more."

"Like what?" Bruin demanded.

"Like Avion..."

"Oh no!" he shot back. "Don't start that again, Mick! Jesus..."

The two men sat in silence for a moment, shuffling uncomfortably in their chairs. Millian's usual sallow complexion had begun to flush noticeably. He felt hot and angry, but also determined to keep a lid on it in front of his boss.

Millian tried a different tack. "Listen, Manny, just take a few things into consideration, okay? Just a few?"

Bruin nodded, reluctantly, and sighed. He didn't want to hear this again, but he really had no choice. It was a matter of friendship.

"Okay," Mick began. "Cathy lived on the next block from Avion. She had a routine that never varied. I mean, *never*. She attended SRJC, just like Avion. She lived there and went to school for a year and a half, plenty of time for Avion to become aware of her and get to know her habits inside out. She was bright, bubbly... hell, she was beautiful — a good target. He would have seen her in the neighborhood; he would have seen her on campus, and he would have had an eye for her. He would have known all about her routines." Millian took a long breath and waited, searching Bruin's face for some response. There was none. He moved on.

"Then there's the rope, Manny. The clothesline rope that he used to strangle her. Avion has that stuff around his cars, his boxes, hell, even around his damn pants legs. How coincidental is that!?"

"All right, Mick, all right," Bruin answered. "That rope means nothing and you know it. If you're going to rely on the rope, you might as well look at the other 50,000 folks in town who use it. As far as Avion's proximity to her — his apartment — the school thing, yeah, well... Okay, it's interesting but it doesn't mean squat. There's nothing for us to do with it, Mick! The stuff that really counts — the forensics, the crime scene, the motives, and any background connections — we have nothing on any of that. You've been all over this thing and so have I. There's nothing to tie Avion and Alverson together. Nothing!"

Millian dropped his head and looked away, unwilling to meet his friend's angry, frustrated stare. He had heard it all before and there was no point in arguing the logic of it. There wasn't any. All he had to go on was instinct, and that wasn't the strongest weapon in his arsenal.

One more try. One more.

"Listen, Manny, can I tag him for a while... on my own time?" he mumbled in a childish voice. "Can I just dog him a bit more, this time for *us* and not for Lionell?"

Bruin sat back in his chair and put a hand over his eyes. What his friend wanted was way off base. They were already bordering on harassment from months of Millian's nearly constant surveillance. All of which had come to nothing. The last thing that Bruin wanted was for this kind of activity to blow up on both of them. What bothered him most was the fact that Mick had this guy Avion stuck so far up his ass that he was going blind. The only argument for letting Millian go back to the trough with Avion was his own cop sense. He had to agree; Byron Avion was one heck of a suspicious guy. But, was that good enough?

"You just *watch* him, Mick, right?" It wasn't a question. "I mean, you stay out of his face, away from his door, and away from him. No confrontations. No conversations. You do it all from a distance, right?"

Millian nodded so rapidly and so hard that his teeth must have rattled inside his head. "That's not a problem, Manny. Hands off. I've got the message. I promise."

Mick Millian's life went from complex to chaotic as a spotty spring bumped and rolled into a hot, dry, and unexpected summer. When he wasn't working his usual overstuffed caseload at the SCCID, Mick spent as much time as he could with Bill Calley, trying to help his oldest friend climb out of the abyss created by his daughter's disappearance. Then there was Byron Avion to think about. There was always Avion to think about.

Bruin's message to his colleague had been clear enough. Mick could keep an eye on Avion, but it had better be done on his own time and it had better be a discreet, distant eye. Mick's nemesis had already made several phone calls to the SCCID and a local judge, angrily complaining about what he saw as Millian's repeated acts of harassment. There had been a considerable flap about it, but no administrative action — just a few stern warnings from above and Bruin's angry outburst.

However, by the spring of 1972, most of the concern had died down. Sam Lionell was out of the picture for a while, so he hadn't been telephoning Bruin to find out what Avion was up to. There were now more than 2,000 suspects under consideration in the

Zodiac investigation and that was keeping everyone in the San Francisco area very busy. The SFPD wasn't showing much interest in Avion these days, probably because of the sheer number of other suspects and all those wasted months dogging him with nothing to show for it. This left only Mick Millian.

Just like the previous year, Millian made little real headway by dogging Avion. The big man kept to his customary, bizarre routines. He continued to attend classes at the SRJC, work his janitorial job a few nights a week, and go on his strange, late-night car-hopping jaunts to who-knows-where. From time to time, Avion would disappear for a few days, as he always had, and then suddenly show up back at his apartment, often carrying one or two cardboard boxes carefully tied with white nylon rope. Millian was especially careful to keep his distance and stay well out of sight. In fact, he took some precautions that would eventually lead him down a twisted, unexpected course.

Mick often talked to Bill Calley about his unofficial surveillance assignment. Just as Bill needed to discuss his fears and how deeply he missed his daughter, Millian also needed someone close to lean on. Avion had become the detective's curse for reasons that he could not identify, understand, or even begin to articulate. Like Bill, Mick needed a way to release the frustration that had overtaken him. For those few months, the two men grew even closer than they had already been. They shared the most painful, most unreachable parts of their souls in a series of late night conversations, usually punctuated with Jack Daniels or Red Chicken Leg Beer from the local brewery.

Millian had helped his friend in many important ways: organizing the volunteers to search for Elaine, keeping both families informed about the progress of the investigation, and working with the media to ensure that the story of the girls would stay alive as long as possible. Now, Bill could help his dearest friend in return, although in much smaller ways.

Since Avion had become all too familiar with Mick's own vehicle, a new look was in order. Bill owned a gray, nondescript, 1968 Pontiac sedan — just the kind of vehicle that faded into the background of virtually any neighborhood. It was especially effective for late-night surveillance and, best of all, it was unknown to Byron Avion. So, Mick asked his good friend if they could swap cars from time to time. "Anytime," was the answer.

Occasionally, Millian would ask Bill if he could borrow a dark overcoat, or even a raincoat, although it usually wasn't chilly or rainy when he made the request. At times it would be a hat or cap, or a black or brown pullover sweater. These little favors were nothing to Bill, at first. Over time, however, Mick's requests stirred an understandable curiosity in his friend and it was inevitable that the detective would eventually tell Bill Calley everything, including his adventures with — and his most far-flung suspicions about — the enigmatic Byron Avion. Despite these conversations, neither man seriously considered Avion as a suspect in the disappearance of Elaine Calley or Mary Spooner. There was no reason for either of them to make such a connection, until Bill Calley and Paul Buchette had their fateful conversation in July. It was that nearly forgotten image of a banged and battered green Volkswagen sitting by the curb near the skating rink that would change everything.

"Mick, Hi, I'm really sorry to bother you at work." Bill Calley's voice was tense and tentative. Millian pulled the handpiece tight against his ear.

"No, not a problem, Bill. It's never a problem. What's up?"

"Well, Mick, I had a conversation with Paul Buchette a while ago. Do you remember him?"

The detective sat back in his chair and rubbed his forehead with two fingers, as if trying to summon a genie from inside his skull. The name was certainly familiar.

"Yeah, I think so... he's the old guy who owns the grocery store across the street from the skating rink, right? Is that who you mean?"

"That's him."

"Well, yeah, I recall that he was interviewed more than once..."

"He was," Calley interrupted. "And I talked to him a few times myself, Mick. Today, he gave me something new — something that I hadn't heard about before, and it stuck in my mind. Maybe there's something here, maybe not. Anyway, I thought you ought to hear about it."

"Okay..."

"On the day that Elaine and Mary disappeared, Buchette saw a guy in a green Volkswagen. He had been parked up the block from the skating rink for an hour or so before the girls came out. When he last saw them, the two were heading toward the Volkswagen. Now, Buchette didn't see Elaine or Mary talk to the guy in the car. He didn't even see them near it, really. But he thought it was strange, that guy sitting out there for so long."

Millian yanked his chair forward, slamming it into the desk and spilling the remains of a coffee cup. The detective knew that car. He *knew* who the driver was.

"Mick, you there?"

"Ah... yeah, Bill, I'm here. Listen, what else did Buchette tell you? Get a license number of the car? A description of the driver? What else?"

Bill also went silent. He had hit on something. It was obvious in Mick's voice.

"This means something, doesn't it Mick? There's something here, isn't there?"

"I'm not sure. Maybe... Tell me what else Buchette said."

"No numbers on the car. In fact, he hadn't even remembered the VW until something I said triggered it. All he could tell me was that the guy sat there for a long time."

"What did he look like? Did Buchette say?"

"Couldn't see him, but he got the impression it was a pretty big guy. Listen, Mick, what's going on? Tell me!" Bill's tone was strained, demanding.

"I can't now, Bill. Not here. I'll come over this evening. Let's just say that Buchette's description of the car has given me some ideas. Can we leave it until tonight, Bill?"

There was no answer.

"Bill?"

"Yeah, yeah... It's this guy Avion, isn't it? That's who you've got in mind, isn't it?"

"We'll talk tonight, Bill. I'll let you know tonight, alright?"

Millian heard the line slip away with a distant, disturbing click.

Gone to Ground

By the first week of August 1972, Jacqueline Avion had been settled in her new home on Callihan Creek Road for the better part of a year. She had resumed her old habit of traveling as often as possible, usually out of the country and usually for a month or more at a time. She was rarely at home that year and the place stood lifeless except for the erratic attention paid to the front and side lawns by the hired gardeners. The lights were never turned on, the neighbors were endlessly suspicious of the place, and people talked of the halcyon days when Sam and Maggie Pinelli lived there.

Why Jacqueline had moved to Santa Rosa in the first place was a mystery. The location was an unlikely one for a single, middle-aged, lifelong city-dweller who craved the good life and showed no interest in family. Sonoma County was beautiful and serene, but it was still remote and backward by San Francisco standards. She certainly hadn't come to town because of her son, Byron. By all accounts, she had always stayed as far away from him as possible, even during those periods when he lived with her. Still, she was drawn to the same location in which her son lived, and no one had a good explanation for that. In a bizarre, unfathomable way, she had always been drawn to Byron.

Since she moved to the area in the fall of 1971, Mick Millian only saw his nemesis at his mom's house three or four times. On those occasions, Avion would drive the fifteen blocks to Callihan Creek Road on a Sunday afternoon, stay with Jacqueline for an hour or two, and then leave. The visits seemed uneventful, except for one small point: Avion would always bring along a cardboard box tied with white nylon rope. When he left, the boxes would stay.

Millian was beside himself about those boxes and what they contained. He wanted nothing more than to get inside Jacqueline Avion's house, talk to her, and find a way to get a look. But his boss had made it clear that he had better keep his distance. Mick rightfully interpreted that advice as applying to Mom, too. So he waited, and watched, and waited some more.

A week after Bill Calley's conversation with Paul Buchette, Millian was sent to San Diego for a law enforcement conference. He was away for six days, supposedly enjoying the warmth, sun, and camaraderie in that city's beautiful Mission Bay District. Bruin had signed him up for the conference. Manny was sure that it would do Mick a world of good to get away from Santa Rosa and his obsession with Byron Avion. Ironically, it was during that trip south that Avion did Mick a big, unintentional favor. Or so it seemed.

On the morning of Millian's third day in San Diego, Avion came storming into the SRPD Central Station to report that his beloved Volkswagen had been broken into and vandalized. The enraged victim demanded to speak to the lieutenant of the shift, claiming that he knew who had broken into his car and screaming about justice. According to Avion, the culprit was the same SCCID officer who had been following and harassing him for nearly a year — Mick Millian. Now the detective had gone too far, and Avion wanted retribution. To make matters worse, this cop-turned-criminal had left a note behind in the victim's car — a handwritten, threatening note.

Avion demanded that an investigation be opened and Millian be immediately arrested and charged. As to the personal property that was stolen from the VW, the victim was very vague — almost disinterested. No, there was nothing too important, he kept repeating. In fact, when it came time to complete the incident report, Avion left that part of the questionnaire blank. What concerned him most was the note. He wanted something done about that, and he wanted it done now!

It took the SRPD lieutenant nearly an hour to calm Avion down. Finally, he was able to help Avion complete his report, bag the note that the complainant had discovered on the front seat of his Volkswagen, and arrange to send a patrolman out to the scene of the crime. The VW was parked in its customary location, about a block away from Avion's apartment. The window on the passenger's side had been broken inward and the interior of the little car was in shambles. Someone had obviously taken the time to go through the inside of the car in detail.

According to the victim, the assault on his VW must have taken place between two and seven o'clock that morning. Avion repeatedly assured the officer that there was no point in worrying about what was taken. He never kept anything of value in the car anyway. He just wanted Millian arrested and taken off the streets.

The patrolman took careful notes, asked all the right questions, snapped off a few photographs, and departed with Avion screaming in his ear that the VW should be dusted for fingerprints to prove that Millian was the culprit. The demand was dutifully ignored.

That afternoon, Manny Bruin got a call from the SRPD, informing him of Avion's report and the accusations that he had leveled against Millian. The SRPD file was packed up and brought to his office early that evening. To the SRPD, this was nothing more than a routine car break-in, except for the fact that a fellow officer had been named in the report. Besides that, the guy who reported the incident had been a real pain in the ass — a demanding, argumentative son-of-a-bitch. The SRPD was more than happy to pass the matter on to the SCCID.

Bruin had a much different reaction to the report. He was confused and worried. Why was Avion pointing the finger at Millian? Was it just because Mick had been dogging him for so long? Was it retribution? There was no way that Mick could have been the one who rifled through that VW. He was in San Diego. What in the heck was going on?

The case file was a simple one. It included a report summary that had been written out by the SRPD lieutenant who had interviewed Avion, several Polaroid photos of the VW with the broken window, an incident report filled out by Avion, a typed referral to the SCCID, and the note that had been found on the front seat of the car. It was the note that grabbed Bruin's attention, and the unmistakably familiar block printing that left him speechless:

> THIS IS <u>YOUR</u> KILLER SPEAKING.
> THIS IS JUST THE FIRST.
> THERE WILL BE MORE TO COME.
> REMEMBER LB?
> YOU SHOULD NOT HAVE LEFT YOUR TRADEMARK.
> DO NOT TURN YOUR BACK.

Manny was stunned at what he saw on the irregular-sized, white sheet. The letters had been meticulously scripted with a blue, felt-tip pen. The lines of text were perfectly straight and even, yet obviously formed by hand. To his untrained eye, the characters on the page seemed identical to the letters that Sam Lionell had shared with him the previous year. Even the phraseology seemed right, especially the opening line. The reference to "LB" could have been "Lake Berryessa," the scene of one of Zodiac's most brutal attacks. Bruin knew that Zodiac had left his cross-hair signature and a brief note behind that day, scrawled in felt tip pen on the driver's door of one of his victim's cars. It was possible that this note was penned by Zodiac! But if it was, why did he have such an interest in Avion? Why would he care about this battered VW? If Avion was truly a suspect in the Zodiac investigation, what did this mean? Was he trying to throw suspicion away from himself by creating this whole break-in? None of it made sense, especially Avion's behavior in reporting the crime. According to the SRPD summary, Avion's attitude that morning was, "furious and in fear that he had been targeted for death."

The good news for Bruin was that Mick Millian could not have been involved in the incident. He was in San Diego with 400 other cops and their families. There was even more good news, but it took Bruin a few moments to recognize it. The incident with the VW could open the book a little wider on Avion. It meant that the SCCID had some legitimate reason to poke around in the big man's life, just a bit, to see what he had been up to. However, it was obvious that Millian had to be kept off the case. If Avion was convinced that Mick had broken into his car and threatened his life, then Bruin had to keep his detective even farther away than before. The person for the job was Bruin himself. He would investigate it just as Avion had reported it: an accusation against a fellow

SCCID officer that needed to be looked into. The sticky issue was the note. What to do with it? How to handle it? What it meant.

It was *possible* that the note left in Avion's VW was the real thing. It was possible, but unlikely, and Bruin knew it. Most of the Zodiac letters had been well publicized in the San Francisco *Chronicle*, including photos and photocopies of the original documents. Anyone who was interested enough in copying Zodiac's style could have easily gathered what they needed from the newspaper reports. The question was why anyone would go to the trouble. Why would anyone want to do this, and why would they target Avion for their bizarre fun and games? Then, there was the small matter of Sam Lionell and his interest in Avion. There was no way that Manny could cut him out of the VW incident, especially if the impossible proved to be right and the note had really been written by the Zodiac.

Bruin called Paul Fiorelli of the SCCID's forensic unit late that evening, summoning him away from an intimate dinner with his wife to appear at the detective's office. When Paul arrived, Bruin showed him the note, which he had carefully placed in a tagged SCCID evidence bag. What he wanted from Paul was simple but vital. Were there any prints on the note? Did this handwriting match that on the Zodiac letters? He handed the technician a stack of photocopies of known Zodiac letters — the same ones that Lionell had shared with him. Those, he told Paul, would provide the control group for his handwriting comparisons.

Then, the kicker: keep all of this to yourself, Paul. Not a word to anyone else about this, and no lab case file!

Fiorelli balked. He was not a handwriting expert. That wasn't in his bag of tricks. He could do the basic forensics, lift any prints, and tell Manny about the paper, pen, and a bunch of other things. But the handwriting was another matter. Besides that, why all the secrecy? That was *not* what he wanted to get involved in.

Bruin closed the door to his office, adopted the fatherly role, and wove a legend for the young technician. He talked about false accusations against a brother officer, the intense Zodiac investigation that was going on in the City, the legendary Sam Lionell, all those murder victims, and everything else that he could think of to persuade Fiorelli that this could be the case of his career. In the end, it worked. Fiorelli agreed to do what Bruin wanted, keep it all to himself, and to at least give the detective his opinion about the handwriting, so long as he could call in an old friend from Sonoma State University to help him look at the note. Fiorelli assured Manny that this would all be done anonymously and his colleague could be trusted. Bruin agreed. Fiorelli would begin right away.

The next step for Bruin was to make a phone call to Sam Lionell. He could have waited until the next morning to call the inspector at his office, but that would have been out of character. Besides, Manny had no idea how many people had seen the Avion note and become curious. Judging by the silence from the SRPD, they had no idea what had potentially passed through their hands. However, Bruin had always erred on the side of caution, and he wasn't about to take any chances now. He dialed Lionell's home number.

"Sam, this is Manny Bruin. Sorry to bother you at home."

"Hey, Manny! Good to hear from you. No, no problem. I'm just sitting around here getting fatter and more lazy by the minute." His voice was upbeat, happy. Bruin could hear the strains of a Rossini opera in the background. Sam sounded a bit happier than normal, Bruin thought.

"You're feeling better these days, Sam?"

"You bet I am! Lots better, Manny. I'm learning how to have a life of my very own for a change. Sometimes getting knocked on your ass is the best thing, you know." Lionell took a long sip of Valpolicella from a short-stemmed glass.

"Yeah, I suppose so, Sam. I wouldn't want you to take that kind of thing too far, though."

Both men chuckled.

"So, Manny, what can I do for you?"

"I've got something here that might interest you, Sam. It's about our old friend Byron Avion. It's an interesting story..."

Bruin went on to give Lionell an outline of what had happened with the VW. He talked about Millian's frustration in dogging Avion. He gave Lionell a full rundown on the note, including his decision to send it to the lab for a non-destructive forensic and handwriting analysis. Bruin never mentioned Millian's suspicions about Avion's possible connection to their local problems. He was careful to keep a low profile throughout the conversation. It was just a courtesy call.

Lionell was hot to get his hands on the note and a little angry that Bruin had given it to his own lab rather than the more sophisticated facilities at the SFPD. Still, Manny said he would immediately fax off a copy of the note and put another one in the overnight mail. When he got the lab results back, he would share them with Lionell and give him the original note so that the SFPD could take a crack at it, so long as all the usual *quid pro quo* courtesies were in place. In the end, Sam seemed happy enough with that arrangement and agreed. He was certainly more pleased than Manny had expected. Perhaps it was Lionell's new, more relaxed attitude. Perhaps it was the wine that he had been drinking.

"Sam, you don't think this note from Avion's car is the real thing, do you?" It was less a question than a statement.

"No, I don't. I guess it's possible, and we should sure check it out, but I don't think so, Manny. I don't think so."

"Listen, Sam, do you think Avion could have written it to throw us off? He could have staged the whole thing, the whole car thing, including the note, just to screw with us."

"He *could* have..." Lionell's voice was serious, a bit caustic. "That's not likely, though. He's not that dumb, Manny. Besides that, I got the impression from what you told me that he was genuinely afraid of what might happen to him. Am I right on this?"

"Yeah, you're right, Sam, I guess. I didn't talk to him, the SRPD did. He could have been faking that too."

Lionell thought for a few seconds, holding the phone close to his lips and breathing noisily. "Tell me this, Manny, do you think Avion is afraid of *anything*? Honestly, does he strike you as that kind of guy?"

Now it was Bruin's turn to be quiet.

"No, Sam, I don't." he whispered. "I don't think that guy is afraid of anything."

"Neither do I," Lionell mumbled back. Then, the kicker: "Manny, you need to look closer to home to find out more about this note. You need to look closer to home."

At noon the next day, Paul Fiorelli was standing in Bruin's office, looking several years older than he had the previous evening. He had worked through the night in the lab and never made it back home to his wife and dinner. Early that morning he had taken the note over to Sonoma State University, where he showed the document to the one man in the county who he was sure could provide a reliable opinion about the handwriting. The two men pored over the note and the photocopies of Zodiac's known letters for several hours. Finally, Fiorelli had all he needed to know and headed back to the SCCID to give Bruin his report.

Fiorelli and his colleague at the University had reached a conclusion that did not surprise Bruin. In fact, he had expected it. The handwriting on the Avion note was close to Zodiac's. It was *very* close, but it wasn't a match. Whoever had written the note that was found in Avion's car was obviously very familiar with Zodiac's hand and style, but it wasn't Zodiac himself. To the casual observer, it could easily be mistaken for the genuine article. However, to someone skilled in handwriting analysis, it was a masterful forgery — nearly a work of art. But not the real thing.

There was even more interesting news on the forensic front. The Avion note had been well-handled. Fiorelli had found a number of latent prints, but none of them were clear and distinct. Since he didn't want to risk destroying the original document, there was little more he could do but photograph the prints. His guess was that the note had been handled by at least four different individuals, which probably included Avion, a few officers at the SRPD, and one or two others. The technician also found something that no one had expected. After analyzing the creases and folds in the note, Fiorelli came to the conclusion that it had originally been rolled up and tied. Whoever discovered the note had untied it, unrolled it, and read it. The reader had made an obvious attempt to work the wrinkles from the page but hadn't done a good job of it. Oh, yes, there was something else. The note could have been tied with a lightweight, nylon cord. Fiorelli had found two strands of this kind of material, which had adhered to the backside of the page. After analyzing them, he was fairly certain that they were from a white nylon cord of some type.

For Bruin, it was another shocker. Avion had made no mention that the note had been rolled up and tied, especially with a nylon cord. He didn't bring any bindings, nylon or otherwise, to the SRPD when he made his report. Avion had only told the officer that he had found the note on the front seat of the car. He gave few other details. This new piece of information sent Bruin's cop antennae into lunar orbit. What if that note *had* been tied with white, nylon rope? What kind of a hidden message was *that* meant to send Avion? No wonder he was so damn scared! No wonder he was convinced that Millian was the culprit! Somehow, this all made sense to Avion, even though it didn't make much sense to Bruin. The next step was obvious: talk to the big man, and do it right away.

There were two days left on Millian's sojourn to San Diego — more than enough time for Bruin to get to Avion and learn what he could. For the rest of that afternoon and into the evening, Manny tried to telephone Avion at his apartment, then at his job, then back at his apartment. He never showed up for work at the grammar school. Every hour, the detective dialed Avion's apartment; every hour the phone rang off the hook. Finally, at around nine that night, after a quick dinner at home, he decided to go to Avion's place and wait. One way or the other, he was determined to get a handle on this thing before Mick got back to town.

As Bruin rolled to a stop across the street from Avion's apartment, he saw the big man hustling down the concrete walkway toward a late-model, windowless brown van parked at the curb. Avion was dressed in his usual dark windbreaker and apparently didn't see the blue sedan across the street. He was moving quickly, taking short determined steps as if he had an urgent agenda.

As Avion approached the intersection of the walkway and the sidewalk, Bruin noticed that he had a fistful of hangered clothes slung over his right shoulder. When he reached the curb, Avion went to the back of the van and pulled open one of its doors. He tossed the bundle of clothes onto the floor of the vehicle, hastily slammed the door, and turned toward the apartment building as Bruin climbed out of his car to intercept him.

"Mr. Avion," the detective said loudly as he crossed the street. "I've been trying to get a hold of you all day."

Avion swung around abruptly and leaned his large frame forward, staring at the man moving toward him. He looked confused and uncertain.

"Who the hell are *you*?" he demanded, angrily dropping his arms to his sides. Then, just as quickly, he recognized Manny Bruin. His posture relaxed and he took a few steps forward, positioning himself between the approaching man and the rear doors of the van, as if to protect it from intrusion.

"Yeah... all right..." he said, matter-of-factly. "Detective Bruin... So, you say you've been trying to get me all day. Now, why would that be, I wonder?" Avion wore that tight, disgusting smile across his broad face.

Bruin continued across the street until he reached the curb, placing himself a few feet away from Avion and the van. "Mr. Avion, you made a police report about your Volkswagen, didn't you? I need to..." Bruin began.

"That was to the Santa Rosa PD, Detective," Avion interrupted. "It wasn't to you."

"Well, Mr. Avion, didn't you mention Detective Millian in your report to the SRPD?"

"You bet I mentioned him! That little shit has been harassing me for too long. Now, he's threatening me and I want it stopped!" Avion's smirk was gone, washed away by a rage that was made even more ominous by the scattered, yellow glow of the streetlight above his head. Instinctively, Bruin moved his right hand a bit closer to the holstered .38-caliber that rested on his hip beneath his sport coat.

"All right, Mr. Avion... I'm here to follow up on your report to the SRPD, to find out what happened. In order to do that, I need to ask you a few questions. I need to find out why you believe that

Detective Millian was involved in this thing, and how." Bruin's voice was low and slow, nearly conciliatory.

Avion shuffled his feet on the sidewalk like an errant child. For a few seconds, he dropped his head, hiding his face. Manny couldn't help but notice that the man's pants legs were loose and flapping against the tops of his boots. He wondered what had happened to the nylon cords that Mick had told him were always there.

"Yeah, okay..." Avion whispered. "We can talk about that. We can talk about Detective Millian, but we can't do it now. It's got to be some other time." With that, the big man turned away from the detective and stepped quickly up the walkway toward his apartment building. Bruin realized that he probably had only one shot at getting his prey to stop before he disappeared inside the building. It wasn't the card he wanted to play so early in the game, but it couldn't wait.

"Mr. Avion, I want to talk about that letter you found in your car. The one that upset you so much — the one that seems to link you to the Zodiac murders." Bruin's voice was loud and demanding.

Avion stopped and whirled around. As he turned, the big man slid his right hand into his jacket pocket. Bruin saw that movement and instantly drew his handgun from his hip. He dropped to a crouching position and took a solid aim at the center of Avion's frame.

"You move a muscle and you'll eat a pound of lead," Bruin growled. "Get your hand out of your pocket! Take it out slowly, along with whatever else is in there and lay it on the ground in front of you. Do it now!"

"Fuck off..." Avion groused back, looking surprised but unafraid.

"Bad decision, Avion... "Manny pulled the hammer back and steadied his aim. He glowered at his target through clenched teeth.

The big man pulled his hand from his pocket and dropped a set of keys to the ground. In a mock gesture of surrender, he thrust both arms high in the air over his head and began to slowly wave them back and forth.

"You take too many chances, Mr. Avion," Bruin said. He released the hammer on his handgun and re-holstered it. "You can put your hands down and pick up your keys. Just take it easy and keep your hands where I can see them."

"Yeah, I take a few chances from time to time," the big man mumbled. He retrieved the keys and held them tightly in his clenched fist. "So do you, Detective."

Bruin decided to ignore the remark. Or was it a threat?

"Do you want to tell me about that note, Mr. Avion? The one you found in your car?"

"I didn't write it," came the reply. "I know that's what you're thinking, but I didn't write it. Detective Millian wrote that note."

"He couldn't have... He was out of town when all that happened."

Avion studied the detective's face, looking for any indication of a lie. The big man's expression suddenly flattened, then became dark. For the first time, he looked worried.

"You're not covering for him, are you? You wouldn't do that, would you?"

Bruin shook his head from side to side.

"Oh, Jesus..." Avion mumbled. He stood silent, looking down at his boots, hiding his face again. Bruin thought that he saw his left hand begin to tremble.

"Mr. Avion, I want to know about that note," Bruin pressed.

No reply.

"I want to know about that note and anything else that you found with it," he repeated, this time in a softer tone.

"I'm moving, Detective. I'm getting out of here *now*. No more questions! I have nothing else to tell you."

Avion whipped around and headed for the apartment building, leaving Bruin alone on the sidewalk. He waited there for a few minutes to see if the man would return. Then, Bruin went back to his car, where he waited for nearly an hour. Avion never reappeared.

Two days later, Millian was back on the job with an in-basket that should have belonged to three detectives. That night, he and

Bruin had dinner at Gratelli's Restaurant near the SCCID office. It had always been Millian's favorite place, especially when someone else paid. Manny obliged and brought his friend up to date on everything that had happened while he was in San Diego, including his strange encounter with Byron Avion. From Bruin's point of view, it was an uncomfortable few hours that he spent with his friend that evening. Mick was uncharacteristically quiet, almost sullen. He asked few questions, even about Avion. When Manny finally pressed him to find out if anything was on his mind, Mick claimed that he was just tired from the trip and wanted to get home, get some sleep, and get back to his usual routine. San Diego had been more of a hassle than a good time. He was glad to be back home, but tired, very tired.

They parted company at about nine o'clock and Manny went directly home. Mick didn't. He went to see his old friend Bill Calley, to talk about Volkswagens, notes, and nylon ropes.

Into the Storm

Summer had slipped into fall and now it was nearing Thanksgiving. At first, the days were hot and dry; then they slithered into breezy and comfortable, and finally bounded into blustery and wet. This was nothing out of the ordinary for Northern California. But to Manny Bruin, it felt vaguely ominous. Most everything did.

As far as Bruin knew, Byron Avion could have dropped off the face of the earth. For months, his name never crossed the detective's desk, although it was often on his mind. Millian hadn't said much about Avion either. In fact, he hadn't said much about anything, but he did keep an eye on Jacqueline's house, just to see if Avion was still making his Sunday visits. He wasn't.

By the end of summer, Avion's apartment had been rented to a tawny, 19-year-old SRJC co-ed from Eureka. She had the good taste and sense to immediately repaint the walls, at her own expense. They were now a warm, pleasing tan, and the apartment was filled with predictable, starving-student furniture. But nothing she did could diminish the impact of that shag carpet.

At the same time that Avion abandoned his apartment, he quit his janitorial job at the Del Bridge Elementary School and dropped his classes at SRJC without saying a word to anyone. The green

VW that had always been parked down the block was never seen again, and the brown van had also evaporated. So had Avion's other cars. So had Avion.

In the City, Sam Lionell was finally back on the job, working as frenetically as ever. By now, it was well into the fall; it was cold and rainy across Northern California, and foggy and depressing in the City. There had been no word from Zodiac all year, and news of the ongoing investigation had all but disappeared from the pages of the San Francisco *Chronicle*. The task force that had been assigned to the case, which once numbered nearly 250 officers, began to dwindle. By Halloween, one of Zodiac's favorite holidays, it sported less than twenty-five investigators. The population of the Bay Area, which had once been universally seized with Zodiac paranoia, had regained its former footing and perspective — somewhat.

In Santa Rosa, the Calley and Spooner families remained publicly optimistic about their missing daughters, although the media showed little sustained interest in the case. Privately, the families had resigned themselves to what had long been obvious to the law enforcement community: Mary and Elaine wouldn't be coming home. What mattered most now was to learn what had happened to the girls — to find some closure for their pain and to ensure that justice would flow from the senselessness of their loss. One way or the other, the Calleys and Spooners needed to reclaim their lives. No one understood this more deeply than Mick

Millian. No one was more committed to having this tragedy come to a proper end.

Of all the people who had been devastated by the disappearance, Bill Calley seemed to be the least able to regain his equilibrium. By the end of summer, Calley had reduced his work schedule to four days a week. He had become increasingly withdrawn from his wife and friends, except for Mick, and often spent days away from home. None of this was characteristic, especially the wandering. He would patiently explain to his wife that he loved her but that he needed time away from everyone. He wanted to be by himself, to spend some time camping at his favorite spot on Cazadero Creek, far west of town. He needed more time and space to adjust.

Bill was obviously in tremendous pain. No one wanted to question his need to work things out on his own, especially his family, so no one pushed the issue. Besides, he was in good hands. Millian stayed close to his old friend and reassured the family that everything would work out in the end. They all believed that Bill would eventually come around to his old self. It was just taking some time for that to happen, and they were willing to wait.

On November 1, 1972, Cynthia Turgell was appointed to the position of Chief Medical Examiner for Sonoma County, replacing her retiring boss, Howard Vorhies. She became the first woman to hold that job, and her appointment was an exceptionally popular one. The celebration for Cindy was held at the Eleven Hills

Restaurant, just east of town, nestled in the hills not far from where Cathy Alverson's body had been discovered. The event was held on the Friday evening following her promotion. Every cop from the SRPD, SCSO, and the SCCID was in attendance, including Manny Bruin, his wife Cecelia, and Mick Millian. Some 150 officers, predominately men, took over the entire restaurant, bar, and dance floor for the evening.

Turgell proved to be an outstanding guest of honor, easily keeping pace with the macho contingent and dispensing round after round of black humor, a popular law enforcement commodity. It was certainly a memorable night, for those who could remember it.

Then, the fun ended. The rainy season came full-force, and all hell broke loose.

November 1972
West Santa Rosa

Leslie Buono was a restless, frustrated, sometimes enraged 13-year-old. She was also charmingly petite, dark-haired, pretty, and mature beyond her years. As with so many kids her age, Leslie's family had been ripped apart by a bitter divorce preceded by years of arguing and relentless tension. At the age of ten, she was left fatherless without any reasonable explanation. Leslie's mom was relegated to a life of survival existence that only a single mother could truly appreciate.

At the age of thirty-six, Pam Buono looked to be well into her forties. She had no immediate prospects for a man, nor did she want one. Pam was bitter, and, like her eldest daughter, often angry for no discernable reason. She had three children: Leslie, the oldest; Marian, who was 11; and Michael, who was eight. Pam worked a 50-hour week as an underpaid desk clerk in one of Santa Rosa's lesser hotels, which left her little time for her children and none for herself. Any financial support from her ex-husband, who had once been a reasonably well-off commercial fisherman, was completely out of the question. Three years earlier, he had taken off for parts unknown.

At a time in her life when Leslie most needed the emotional support and guidance of both parents, she found herself trying to take on the role of surrogate mother to her two younger siblings. Pam desperately needed Leslie's help and often felt that her eldest daughter wasn't pulling her weight. Leslie desperately needed to talk to her mom, share secrets, be loved, and be appreciated for who she was becoming. None of that happened. The inevitable spats between mother and daughter soon exploded into hurtful words, then into daily arguments, and finally coalesced into a cold, silent distance.

On a drizzly, miserable Wednesday in early November, Leslie finally made up her mind. She had been thinking about nothing else for weeks, maybe months. She wouldn't be going to Rosemont Junior High that day, or any other day. No one at the school really cared about her anyway. She wouldn't have to worry about Marian and Michael, and what they were doing or not doing. She would no longer have to share the few items that she could rightfully claim as hers; she wouldn't have to be crammed into a narrow, drafty, embarrassing two-bedroom apartment. Most important, she wouldn't have to fight with her mom anymore. Leslie would be heading south today, to somewhere she had never been, to somewhere warmer and more inviting — maybe even Los Angeles. Maybe even Hollywood!

She gathered a loose bundle of her favorite clothes, her forlorn collection of cheap jewelry, and two of her favorite paperbacks — both love stories — and stuffed everything into a blue canvas bag with brown plastic handles. Leslie wrote a brief note to her mother, scrawled in an overly large, almost childlike hand on the back of a greasy receipt for pizza delivery. Yes, she loved her. She would be back, so please don't worry.

She left the note on the kitchen table and walked out the door, carefully pushing her apartment key through the mail slot so that her mom would find it that evening. She wouldn't be needing it. Leslie Buono headed on foot toward Highway 101. She would never be seen alive again.

One month later, to the day, a pair of hikers were wending their way along Burnside Creek, about a mile from where Cathy

Alverson's body was discovered that April. It was a brisk, unusually bright morning for early December, and the two hikers were making excellent headway toward their destination at the east end of Santa Rosa. Along the way, they approached a steep embankment where the creek flowed underneath the raised roadway. In order to traverse the area, the pair had to scale their way up the embankment, walk across the two-lane road, and make their way down the other side to the creek bed. It was on the way down the west embankment that they saw the body of a young woman strewn crazily along the edge of the creek. Next to her lay an empty blue canvas bag with brown plastic handles. Frightened, but still relatively composed, the pair sprinted more than a mile to the nearest farmhouse to report their discovery.

Leslie Buono became Cynthia Turgell's first homicide case as the County's new medical examiner. She was on the scene at Burnside Creek within an hour of the discovery, along with Bruin, Millian, and the usual cadre of SRPD and SCSO personnel. Unlike Cathy Alverson, this victim was clothed, although it was obvious that all her personal effects were missing. Like Alverson, Leslie's earrings — a simple pair of silver hoops — had been ripped from her ears. There was no identification on the victim. From her preliminary examination at the dumpsite, Turgell could tell that the victim had sustained a broken neck and that her wrists had been bound, although the bindings were nowhere to be found.

Everything else would have to wait for an autopsy and the results from the forensics lab.

Late the next afternoon, Bruin learned from Paul Fiorelli at the lab that the identity of the girl at Burnside Creek was Leslie Buono. Turgell concluded that she had died of a broken neck. She had fallen, jumped, or been thrown from the side of the road, down the embankment, and onto the rocky creek bed below. On the way down, her neck snapped. Leslie had also been bound with white nylon rope. Strands of the bindings were still embedded in her wrists. She had not been sexually assaulted or injured in any other way. Beyond that, neither Turgell nor the forensics team had anything important to offer. There were no usable tire tracks in the area, no other evidence around the body, and no witnesses to Leslie's fate. Like the Alverson site, this was a remote location, rarely traveled by anyone other than a few locals. The closest home — the farmhouse from which the hikers had made their telephone call — was well out of sight of the bend in the road where Buono's body was found.

Millian was beside himself about Leslie Buono's abduction and murder. To him, the pattern was obvious. He was convinced that Byron Avion was her killer, and his arguments were beginning to sound more plausible, even to the ever-cautious Bruin. A case file was opened and a quick decision made to throw some additional resources into locating Avion. Bruin would ask for help from the Sheriff's Office, although he knew that the assistance would be minimal and short-lived.

Millian desperately wanted to head this effort, to be in charge of a small task force to hunt the man down and bring him into the box for questioning. Bruin flatly refused. It was still too hot an issue for Millian — still too close to home. Mick was relegated to the sidelines and told to work the case from the inside. From Manny's point of view, his friend seemed to handle the decision well. He nodded and agreed. There was little argument.

The following day, Mick left work early in the afternoon. He wanted to meet with his friend, Bill Calley, about some family matters. Would Manny mind? No, not at all. That afternoon, Mick and Bill piled into the Calley station wagon and headed west, out into the country, to be alone.

One week later, the horror of Mary and Elaine's fate came full circle, only a few days before Christmas, when their remains were discovered by a Sonoma County work crew only a few hundred yards from where Cathy Alverson had been found. The girls had been dumped about 50 feet east of the county road. Their bodies had been covered with thick layers of underbrush ripped from the surrounding area. The work crew had been passing through the area to survey drainage along the embankments and had stumbled across the remains. They were little more than skeletons.

The girls were found lying side-by-side, on their backs, as if they had been carefully staged before they were hidden from view. Over the ten months since their disappearance, the predators and elements had taken a heavy toll. However, the four lengths of nylon rope that lay near the bodies had fared a bit better. Although they were beginning to disintegrate, they remained mostly intact and identifiable.

Word of the gruesome discovery came to Manny Bruin through a telephone call from Lieutenant Oroville of the SCSO just after ten that morning. He had few details to share — just two bodies, only skeletons, had been found off the side of the road, east of town, very close to the Cathy Alverson dump site. Bruin's hands shook uncontrollably as he took the call. He struggled to fight off the nausea that paralyzed his stomach and chest. The detective didn't need further details. He was certain about the identities of the victims. So was Lieutenant Oroville.

Manny raced from the SCCID building, pausing at the dispatch desk to ask that someone track down Mick Millian and let him know what was going on. Millian was somewhere in the field and Bruin wanted his partner to meet him at the crime scene immediately. No, he had no idea where Millian was. Just find him! Get him out there, now!

Turgell had moved even faster than Bruin. She received a call from the SCSO just moments before Manny. At the time, she was meeting with Paul Fiorelli about the Buono case. They were comparing notes, trying to come up with something — anything — that could open up the investigation. In a moment, that was forgotten. Turgell and Fiorelli rushed to the ME van and sped off to the site. Like Bruin, they were certain about the identity of the victims.

By the time Bruin arrived at the site, Turgell and Fiorelli had already left the van and were carefully working their way toward the remains. A uniformed SCSO officer was staking out a wide perimeter, positioning yellow tape to protect the dumpsite. Manny pulled himself out of the sedan and stuffed his frame into a faded blue SCCID windbreaker with huge white lettering on the back. He headed east, off the shoulder of the road, to where Turgell and Fiorelli were standing. A few feet away lay the frail, broken bones that had once been two beautiful young girls. Bruin glanced at Turgell. Huge tears wound their way down her reddened cheeks. He moved closer and put his left arm across her shoulders. She was shaking uncontrollably.

"I'm sorry, Manny," she gurgled. "I'm sorry... Not very professional."

He shook his head and looked over at Fiorelli, who was standing just beyond Cindy. The young man's head had dropped to his chest. He didn't want to look. None of them did.

For a few moments, the three stood there, frozen. The agony of their disappearance had run much deeper than Bruin had expected. It had run to the iron-like core of a seasoned ME and straight into the gut of a practiced cop. It was a horror that they all had suspected they would encounter someday, but none wanted to have confirmed.

"All right, Manny," Turgell croaked, pulling away from his arm. "Let's get on this thing. I, for one, want to get this motherfucker!"

Bruin had never heard her use anything close to that language. He never would again.

The little woman with the red tackle box snapped herself to attention and began her practiced ritual. Fiorelli tagged behind her in silence, working the perimeter of the site for any evidence that might have survived the seasons, meticulously placing this and that into brown paper bags. Manny went back to his car, retrieved the Polaroid camera from the trunk, and returned to take as many photographs as he could, from every conceivable angle. As he finished the last shot, he caught sight of another blue sedan pulling to a stop across the road from where he stood. It was Mick Millian, and he wasn't alone.

Bill Calley, who had been riding in the passenger's seat, jumped from the vehicle and bounded across the road in Manny's direction. Quickly, the detective scurried across the shoulder and positioned himself in front of Calley, blocking his way.

"Jesus, Manny!" Bill exclaimed. "Is it them? Are they the ones?"

Bruin put his right hand against Calley's shoulder, more to keep him at bay than to reassure him. Bill was pressing forward, trying to get around Bruin to where the remains lay. Behind his glasses, Calley's blue eyes had turned frothy and tight. He looked like a man possessed.

"We don't know, Bill. We don't know anything yet." Bruin's voice was strained and crackling.

Calley continued to push forward, sending Bruin back a step and forcing him to drop the camera and use both hands to keep him back. He was surprised at the smaller man's strength.

"Listen, Bill!" Manny ordered, "You've got to let us do our work here! If we find anything, we'll let you know. You *know* that we will let you know!"

Calley's forward momentum suddenly eased, as if his body had been drained of its life force. He turned to look directly at Bruin, his glasses fogged, his eyes wet but still enraged.

"I know it's them, Manny..." he whispered. "I know it is."

Bruin stared back at Calley, trying to imagine his suffering. This was the last thing that should have happened — Calley being at the scene. It could do nothing but make things worse. Damn Millian! How could he have been so stupid!

"Listen, Bill," Manny said gently. "We're not going to keep anything from you, I promise. If it's them, we'll let you know. We'll let you know right away. We'll take care of it, you know that." His voice quivered with emotion.

Calley nodded and tried to peer around Bruin's shoulder to where Turgell and Fiorelli were working. Manny quickly stepped in front to block his view.

"Bill, why don't you let Mick take you home? He can stay with you if that would help. I'll contact both of you right away, as soon as I learn anything at all. Why not do that, Bill? It's better for all of us."

Calley dropped his shoulders, then his head. He had given up. Without speaking, he turned away and shuffled toward Millian's car.

"That son-of-a-bitch is going to pay for this, Manny, even if it takes the rest of my life," he said, without looking over his shoulder.

Calley crossed the road and pulled open the passenger's door. He slung himself onto the seat, slammed the door, and stared down at the floorboard.

Bruin began walking forward quickly and caught Mick in the middle of the road. Without thinking, he stuck out a burly hand and pushed his friend hard on the chest, sending him back a few steps. Bruin's face was flushed with rage, his fists clenched.

"Stupid, insensitive thing to do, Mick! That's the kind of shit I'd expect from a rookie!"

Mick pulled back a step further and began to speak.

"Just shut up, Mick! I don't want to hear a word from you! You get Bill Calley home and you do it now! Then, when I call you, you had better come up with a good reason why you brought him here in the first place!"

Bruin whipped around and stomped off to the shoulder of the road, leaving Millian alone. The younger detective glanced around nervously at the others. Had they heard what Bruin said? Had Turgell and Fiorelli heard the confrontation? How could they not? Millian turned and slithered toward his sedan. He slid behind the wheel, fired it up, and sped away from the shoulder, spewing tiny, angry pellets of granite and clay across the road.

As Manny approached Cindy Turgell, he could see that the pain had returned to her face. Her cheeks were dry, but just barely. She turned and looked up at him, then in the direction where Millian had been parked.

"Was that Mr. Calley?" she asked with a look of embarrassment. "Was that the dad?"

Manny nodded painfully.

"Oh, Christ..." she muttered. "Bad scene all the way around..." Turgell turned away for a moment, snapped off her latex gloves, and motioned toward Fiorelli, who was still working near the skeletons. He joined her and Bruin.

"Listen, Manny, I have a problem here," she began. "I'm over my head on this. The victims are so decomposed that we're only dealing with bones here — skeletons. That's out of my league, Manny, and I need some help. What I'm suggesting is that we photograph the site as well as we can, have Fiorelli bag up everything that he can find, retrieve the remains and take them to the lab, and then call in an anthropologist I know to look at the skeletons. Maybe, together, we can come up with a cause of death and something on the forensics front. What do you think?"

Manny nodded, slowly, almost absently. He had nothing to say; nothing came to mind. Whatever Turgell thought best was okay with him. All he wanted to do was get the hell out of there — be alone for a while. Cindy saw that; she read it in his face and in his body language.

"Okay, Manny. We can take the scene from here. No need for you to hang around. Just leave me your camera and I'll call you when I get back to the lab. Will that work for you?"

Bruin said nothing, but he moved close and gave her a light hug before he left. Thank God for that runt with the red hair and tackle box. She was a rare one.

Nothing in living memory so grabbed the attention of Santa Rosans as the discovery of Mary and Elaine's remains. These two girls had become the town's daughters — representatives of a loved and endangered generation. The *Journal* ran a quick series of articles about the girls and their disappearance. A memorial service was held three days after their bodies were found. More than 3500 townsfolk attended. Most of them had never met Mary or Elaine, but they knew that what had happened to the Spooner and Calley families could have happened to any of them. At the service, Bill Calley spoke briefly and movingly. He explained that a formal funeral would have to wait until the SCCID and the ME had done their work. He thanked everyone, especially his best friend Mick Millian and the lead investigator in the case, Manny Bruin. He cried openly. So did many others.

Manny and Mick arrived at St. Emanuel's Catholic Church in separate cars. They nodded a brief greeting to each other but stood apart throughout the service. There was still much to talk about. Millian had never given his partner a good reason for bringing Calley along that morning, and Bruin had a hard time forgiving an act so insensitive. Mick had never told Manny why his brain had been so out of gear that day, how he had managed to gather Calley up so quickly and get him to the site. For the first time in their long friendship, Bruin felt a gnawing sense of doubt about his partner. But there would be time to talk about that later. For now, he wanted to find out what had happened to the girls, and why, and who.

Cindy Turgell had recruited Dr. Victor Stinesky, a professor of anthropology at San Francisco University, to help her with the remains of Mary and Elaine. Identifying the girls had been a straightforward process, as both had lived in Santa Rosa and both had local dental records. However, the fact that only skeletons remained at the dumpsite made it impossible for either Turgell or Stinesky to pinpoint a cause of death. Both agreed that Mary and Elaine had probably been murdered elsewhere and transported to the location at which they were discovered nearly a year later. Whoever brought them there had made a considerable effort to conceal the bodies.

The only forensic evidence was a few pieces of decomposing white nylon rope. This seemed to connect the girls' murder to the other Highway 101 victims, despite the fact that the manner in which the bodies were discarded was very different. Once again, without any kind of hard evidence, it was impossible for Bruin to get his investigation off first base. However, he was now convinced that a serial killer was working the area. The murderer clearly had a general preference for young women or girls who hitchhiked on Highway 101.

How, then, did Mary and Elaine fit into the picture? That was Bruin's immediate problem. Perhaps the girls were his first victims. Maybe he took them before he had settled on an MO that involved hitchhikers.

Bruin had the beginning of a theory. So did Turgell and Millian. Manny believed that they were dealing with two killers, not one. The first — the man who claimed Mary and Elaine — was a different predator than the man who abducted and murdered the hitchhikers. The first killer was a resident of the area, had seen the girls on many occasions, and had planned his attack carefully, including where he would dump their bodies. Bruin's second murderer was not a resident of the immediate area but knew it well. His work probably took him through Santa Rosa, on a regular basis. Perhaps he was a truck driver, or a salesman.

Turgell disagreed. She was convinced that they were dealing with one serial killer. From a forensics point of view, she found it impossible to overlook the white nylon rope common to all the murders. She agreed that the rope was an everyday item. But why was the killer so careful in not leaving any traces behind, except for the rope? It didn't make sense, unless the rope was a part of the killer's ritual, a way of implanting his trademark on the crimes.

She agreed that this was a man who was familiar with the town and the surrounding area. But, she argued, he didn't have to live in Santa Rosa. All that was needed was some ongoing connection, like a relative who lived in town, or a job. Turgell believed that he would be a large, strong man, perhaps exceptionally strong. Yet he would also be capable of winning the trust of his victims, especially Mary and Elaine. She thought that the killer might have selected them first because he had seen them repeatedly, knew their habits, and possibly even talked to them before. They were the first victims because they were close to him in some way. Then he caught a taste for killing and moved on to safer targets. Who would be a safer target than a lone female hitchhiking along Highway 101?

Millian strongly supported Turgell's argument, but he went further. He was convinced that the man they sought was Byron Avion. Not only did he fit her profile, he also fit many of the points that Bruin had raised. Here was a guy who not only lived in town but also had strong connections here. He held a job in Santa Rosa, attended the SRJC regularly, and had a close relative who now lived here. Avion could well have known all the victims. He could have repeatedly seen the co-eds on campus, watched them, and waited for his opportunity. As for Mary and Elaine, Paul Buchette had seen a green VW in front of the skating rink that day, and Avion had a green VW. The big man was evasive, elusive, and had several vehicles and more than one place that he called "home." Then, there was the white nylon rope — always the white nylon rope. It had been found with each of the victims and was a fundamental part of Avion's existence.

In the end, Bruin had to agree. Avion was looking more and more like their man. But how could they tie him to these killings? Even more troubling was a point that they all agreed on – they hadn't heard the last from this serial killer, and they would probably find more victims.

February 1973
Lynn Howard

Only a few days passed before the Santa Rosa *Journal* jumped into the serial killer speculation game with both feet. Their coverage was generally objective and sensitive to the families of the victims, but the series of articles that ran in late December

1972 and early January 1973 made it clear that the SCCID had no primary suspects in the four murders. Bruin, Millian, and Turgell knew better, but they didn't dare say anything to the press. Four days after Christmas, a lengthy *Journal* article made it clear that hitchhiking along the freeway was a risky undertaking, and spelled out all the gruesome details. It was in that piece that a reporter for the *Journal* gave the unknown fugitive his moniker: The Highway 101 Killer.

Bruin, his wife, and Mick Millian spent New Year's Eve together. It was the first time that the two detectives had socialized since the discovery of Mary and Elaine's remains. Bruin had prepared himself for a tense evening, even though he had been the one to invite Millian to come over. To his relief, the evening went well. After a few rounds of drinks and some light conversation, the two men settled into a comfortable dialogue that ran until nearly two in the morning. They covered every conceivable topic — almost. Both were careful to avoid the incident with Bill Calley, and Millian never mentioned Byron Avion. When they parted that night, it seemed that the wounds were healing.

Bruin took whatever steps he could to narrow the field of suspects in the four murders, but there wasn't much to go on. He and Millian carefully examined every missing person's report for any similarities that might jump out at them. It was clear to both detectives that their killer would probably strike again, but at this point they could do little more than wait.

In the third week of February 1973, a missing person's report crossed Mick Millian's desk. Three days earlier, a missing person's report came out of Humboldt County on a fifteen-year-old girl. Lynn Howard had run away from home, leaving no word with her parents or older brother. The following day, she phoned her home at around noon and told her brother that she was in Santa Rosa. Her plans were to hitchhike south until she reached San Jose, where she would spend some time with her older cousin. Nothing her brother said could convince Lynn to come home, even after he offered to drive immediately to Santa Rosa to pick her up. Lynn was determined to be on her own. She told her brother she loved him, to say the same to their parents, and hung up.

Lynn placed that call from a pay phone at the Greyhound bus station in downtown Santa Rosa. The terminal is located directly underneath a raised portion of Highway 101, with direct access to off ramps heading both north and south. After talking to her brother, Lynn walked underneath the freeway and up the southward ramp. When she reached the shoulder of Highway 101, she stuck out her thumb and was picked up almost immediately by a large man driving a late-model, white sedan.

Lynn climbed into the passenger's seat and spoke briefly to the man behind the wheel before closing the door. The sedan sailed away from the shoulder, moved directly into the fast lane, and sped off, rolling away from the last person who saw Lynn Howard alive: Bill Calley.

Calley was headed home for lunch and had taken Highway 101 south to avoid the usual midday downtown traffic. When he got on, he was frustrated to discover that the freeway was jammed by a detour that had nearly closed the far right lane. Calley first noticed Lynn Howard from several hundred feet away as he sat in stalled traffic in the slow lane. He saw the young, black-haired girl move to the edge of the roadway and wait no more than 30 seconds before the white sedan crossed the lane between two other cars and pulled to a stop just in front of her. The sedan sped away, leaving Bill crawling along, two lanes to the right. There was no chance for him to follow or get a license plate number. In fact, had the witness been anyone other than Bill Calley, the entire incident might have been forgotten.

When Millian saw the report on Lynn Howard, he immediately knew that it was the same incident that Bill Calley had described the day before. Bill was very concerned about what he saw, but Millian had assured him that the incident was probably nothing. Still, he suggested that Bill try to write down as much as he could remember.

In Eureka, Lynn's brother filed a police report on the day she left home and then called the local police to tell them about Lynn's phone call from Santa Rosa. The Eureka PD followed through on the information and phoned the SRPD. They also faxed a copy of the missing person's report down to the SRPD, who had been instructed to forward all such reports to the SCCID. It was an efficient, effective process. It came a day too late to save Lynn Howard's life, but no one would know that for five months.

When Millian saw the report on Howard and realized that his friend, Bill Calley, had been a witness to a possible abduction, he wasn't willing to play the odds. It was unlikely that Bill had seen anything important; it was far more likely that his friend was reacting to his own painful journey. Still, it wouldn't take much for Mick to put the issue to rest.

With a few phone calls, Millian learned about Lynn Howard's destination. Over the next two days, he telephoned Lynn's cousin in San Jose several times, along with her brother in Eureka. By now, the girl should have arrived, but no one had heard from her. After she made that phone call from Santa Rosa — and after she climbed into the white sedan — Lynn appeared to have vanished.

Millian waited another week, just to be sure. He called Howard's cousin and brother every other day. By the end of the week, Mick was convinced that whatever Bill Calley had seen might have been the real thing. It was time to risk Manny Bruin's wrath once more.

To Millian's surprise, Bruin jumped on the Lynn Howard incident with both feet. Besides, they had almost nothing else to go on. This was the first incident in a long time that seemed even remotely connected to the case.

Bruin gave his partner the okay to chase down everything that he could find on Lynn Howard. He was to work with Bill Calley and a sketch artist, try to learn what he could about the white sedan, and work with Howard's brother and cousin to learn everything that he could about Lynn. If the road led to Byron Avion, that would be fine. If not, that would be all right too. So long as it led *somewhere*.

Byron Avion

By early 1973, the SCCID and the San Francisco Police Department had pieced together a tantalizing portrait of Byron Avion's background, although it was punctuated with gaps, inconsistencies, and questions of lifestyle. Sam Lionell had concentrated on Avion's activities around the Bay Area from just before the first Zodiac murder in 1969 until the present. Millian, on the other hand, had burrowed much deeper. He was on the lookout for the subtleties in Avion's life — some critical pattern in his behavior, perhaps a thread of consistency that would tie him more closely to the Highway 101 murders. Avion had become the central mission in Millian's life.

Byron Edmond Avion was born in Los Angeles, in 1934. He was the only son of a career officer in the U. S. Army. Avion's mother, Jacqueline, had never worked and had married her husband as soon as she graduated from high school, at the age of eighteen. Frank Avion, a colonel and intelligence specialist, was eleven years older than his wife and the picture of military stoicism. Lean, very tall, and impassive to a fault, Frank had been among the inner circle of up-and-coming young intelligence officers from his early military days. He was widely recognized as an exceptionally bright man who followed orders and offered few opinions. He was a black hole of information. He absorbed everything, spoke of virtually nothing, and was a master at working behind the scenes in complex intelligence and counterintelligence programs.

All of this mystery seemed to suit the Colonel perfectly and made him an interesting topic of conversation among military wives. On the home front, however, he was little more than a bystander, courteous to his wife but rarely involved in her life or interests. His clear passion was for things unseen, unknowable, top-secret, and vital to the national interest. He was a classic military gentleman with a mission that did not include family.

Typical of a military family, Frank and his wife lived in a variety of locations before Byron arrived on the scene. Many of these early assignments were in the Southeastern states at out-of-the-way installations with undefined missions. None of this went down well with Jacqueline, who thrived on the lure of big cities, glitzy storefronts, and the bustle of people. But she made few complaints to her husband. From her simple, small-town point of view, there really wasn't any point in grousing about her life. At least she had achieved her freedom from a childhood overflowing with constraints and criticisms, and there was always Frank's next assignment to look forward to. Perhaps, one day, it would be in or near a big city.

Then, it happened — the thing that she had always secretly dreaded. She became pregnant. Frank and his wife had talked about having children, but those conversations always seemed more theoretical than real, more distant than imminent. Perhaps it was Frank's lack of enthusiasm about the mundane things in life, like children; perhaps it was Jacqueline's well-hidden desire to avoid having kids around to tie her down. Whichever, she wasn't ready for it, and it changed her both psychologically and physically. Within months, she ballooned from her trim 105-pound, five-foot frame to nearly 160 pounds. She became withdrawn, sullen, unkempt, and as incommunicative as her husband. It was a dangerous time for the Avion marriage, a time when the Colonel's eyes could well have roamed. The partnership was saved by Frank's obliviousness to the changes that had befallen his wife. For those few months, both Frank and Jacqueline tactfully avoided the subject of her pregnancy and did not speak of her once-alluring figure. He just spent more time doing whatever it was that he did.

Then came another change, a new and unexpected assignment for Frank. When Jacqueline was six months pregnant, the Colonel was sent to Los Angeles, a desk job that involved working with defense contractors in Southern California on deployment and intelligence war-game scenarios. Jacqueline could not have been happier.

That year, 1934, her son was born: Byron Edmond Avion. His first name came from her father, a generally hated man when he was alive, but he carried sufficient influence from the grave to command recognition. Byron's middle name was the same as his father's, another concession to lineage. After Byron's birth, Jacqueline quickly trimmed down to her former petite frame, re-established her vivacious appearance and attitude, and established herself with a network of military wives who would be willing to babysit on the days that she was drawn to the big city. It was a good time for Jacqueline, perhaps the best in her life. She had attained one of her great dreams and her young son had become the ward of a community of close-knit, reliable women.

Byron was six years old when the family was ordered to move once again. For Jacqueline, this proved to be an even better turn of events. Frank was assigned to a top-secret code section that was being formed at the San Francisco Presidio, perhaps the most sought-after, prestigious military post in the country. It was more than either Frank or Jacqueline could have hoped for. The Colonel was moving ever deeper into the inner sanctum of intelligence work, which had been his life's ambition since he first enlisted in the Army. Jacqueline, who had always placed San Francisco at the top of her dream cities, had hit the lifestyle jackpot. As for Byron, he was just along for the ride.

In the summer of 1940, the family relocated to the Presidio, where Frank, Jacqueline, and Byron were assigned a private officer's residence nestled in the thick groves of eucalyptus trees covering the base's northern edge. By military standards, it was a plush assignment. For the first time in their lives, they had a spacious private home, and it came with some enviable embellishments, such as a military driver and janitorial services provided by grunt recruits. They settled into their regimen easily and, in the fall of that year, Byron was enrolled in the elementary school on the base.

Life at the Presidio was exceptionally easy by traditional Army standards. The base was essentially a self-contained city that provided every conceivable service to its resident officers and enlisted personnel. One of the oldest army facilities in the United States, the pre-World War II Presidio was a collection of tasteful, wooden-framed buildings, comfortable offices and facilities, enormous warehouses, a six-story hospital, and a century-old cemetery, all of it surrounded by rolling hills populated by thick groves of eucalyptus and redwood. To the casual observer, this semi-open military facility seemed more like a private park perched along the shore of the San Francisco Bay. However, the activities that went on inside those innocuous frame buildings were anything but simple or obvious. In those days, the Presidio was home to a collection of sophisticated intelligence and code-breaking operations that would eventually prove crucial to America's victory in World War II. Frank Avion's role in some of these covert operations would prove to be the pinnacle of his military career, and the probable cause of his premature death.

Jacqueline Avion loved the Presidio assignment in a way that she had never loved anything before. She would venture off base almost every day and spend hours touring the limitless secrets of San Francisco. Jacqueline's father, who had died the same year that her son was born, had left the family more than a little money, which his daughter guarded carefully and never wasted. Her trips to the City were anything but spending sprees. Jacqueline would stroll the crowded streets of downtown or the North Beach district and window-shop for hours on end, fantasizing about faraway, exotic places, and mentally dressing herself in the luxurious garments that she saw in rows of alluring shops. Most days, she would treat herself to an espresso at Gianni's, sometimes accompanied by a sweet roll or a few slices of French bread. Every day, she dreamed, and strolled, and dreamed some more, coming to know the City as well as any native.

In a place like San Francisco, with such extraordinary sensory delights and unlimited sophistication, it's easy to become lost in fantasy and visions of the future. This is what happened to Jacqueline Avion. It was during Frank's assignment at the Presidio that Jacqueline first discovered, then committed herself to, a life of travel and adventure — someday, some way, despite the constant vicissitudes of being a military wife. In San Francisco, she had caught the bigger-better-life bug, the restless, wandering compulsion, and it would stay with her for the rest of her life.

With Frank working odd and long hours, and Jacqueline hopelessly captivated by Baghdad-by-the-Bay, Byron was relegated to an afterthought. To make matters worse, he was not an appealing child to begin with. Even as a toddler, it was clear that Jacqueline's son would someday be unusually big, perhaps even taller than his father's six foot, three inches. However, unlike Frank, who had always been lean and trim, it was obvious that Byron would be a person of girth and fluff. Byron had the shape of a fireplug, although in his early years it was often excused as cute. In his later school years, Byron's spherical figure would be anything but, serving to reinforce his sense of isolation from the rest of the world.

From Jacqueline's point of view, her young son was in good hands at the Presidio. The military provided a comfortable lifestyle for her family, an education for Byron that was better than most, and the safety that was inherent in living on an Army base. When the school day ended, there were even military personnel who were assigned to stay with the youngsters until it was time to drive them home. In the late afternoon, a small gray bus was dispatched to pick the kids up at the school daycare center and deliver them to the doorstep of the officers' quarters. It all seemed perfect to Jacqueline, and she learned to abandon all worry about her offspring. But for Byron, it was not so idyllic.

By the time Jacqueline's son reached the fifth grade he had become the favorite target of a crusty, overstuffed staff sergeant who was in charge of transportation for the kids at the base elementary school. The balding, forty-something officer quickly realized that Byron was on his own from the time he reached school until late in the afternoon, or sometimes even later. Within a few months of Byron's enrollment in school, the sergeant (call him "Bob") had endeared himself to the Avion family because of his special interest in the new student and the unspoken similarities in their physiques. Whenever Jacqueline was late from her jaunts to the City, an increasingly common occurrence, Uncle Bob would be sure that Byron was not alone and delivered safely to her door as soon as she returned. Whenever Byron scraped his knee or got into a tussle with another kid at school, Uncle Bob would be there to wipe away the tears, tell the young boy a funny story, or just help him idle away the hours until Jacqueline got home. It was during those idle times that Bob molested Byron — repeatedly.

At first, the assaults were rare and relatively subtle; by the fifth grade, they became routine. The little boy said nothing. He never told his parents. He simply came to accept the behavior as the price to be paid for Uncle Bob's attention — the kind of attention that was lacking in the Avion household.

Finally, the abuse came to an end. In the early summer between Byron's fifth and sixth grade, Uncle Bob was transferred to Hawaii. He was never heard from again until he was arrested for molesting a seven-year-old and summarily jailed. However, he had left his mark. It would be three decades before Byron would talk to anyone about those years of sexual abuse, and then he would insist against all reason that his perverse encounters with Uncle Bob numbered only a few.

In 1947, Byron enrolled as a freshman at St. Augustus High School in the Park District of San Francisco. There were no high school facilities at the Presidio, and St. Augustus offered young men the kind of education that could take them to some of America's most prestigious universities, if they had the will to stick with the strict curriculum. Byron did not. Although his IQ was estimated at 135 as he entered high school, he was never able to focus on his classes. In his sophomore year, Avion's grade point average topped out at slightly better than "D." His father was beside himself with disappointment and frustration. In one of his rare moments of family involvement, Frank put the teenager into hard time at home to match the probationary status imposed by the high school. Byron's extraordinary freedom evaporated, and Jacqueline found herself housebound and condemned to the role of warden.

Both Jacqueline and Frank prepared for the worst, expecting their son to be expelled from St. Augustus and permanently set adrift in life. But they were pleasantly surprised. Byron must have received his father's message loud and clear because, by the end of the school year, he was doing better than "B" work and had earned two special recognition awards from the dean for academic performance. As a reward, Frank resumed his former level of disinterest in family affairs and Jacqueline turned her eyes and heart back to the City. Despite this lack of interest, Byron continued to do well in school, although without any friends either at St. Augustus or on the base.

Then came the crash and burn.

In the spring of the following year, Frank Avion died of a massive heart attack. Within two months of the Colonel's funeral, Jacqueline was forced to leave her beloved base. This unexpected eviction significantly rewrote her tightly scripted lifestyle and permanently poisoned her previously forgiving view of the Army. It was not a completely disastrous turn of events, however, because Jacqueline had done well financially. Frank's death swelled her already significant family coffers by some $40,000. She was now able to purchase a modest home in the Potrero Hill District of San Francisco to replace her Presidio quarters. She would miss the free janitorial services and the flawlessly polite driver, but she would make do. The only drawback was that Jacqueline now found herself solely responsible for Byron, and the angry teenager was deteriorating at lightning speed.

After his father's death, Byron's grades dropped drastically and he began cutting classes in favor of drinking cheap wine and generic beer in Golden Gate Park – alone. The dean tried to work with Jacqueline and her son to get him back into the regime of school life, but nothing worked. Preoccupied with their separate fantasies, Byron and his mother seemed completely indifferent to what was going on around them. At the end of his junior year, Byron was summarily expelled with a curt letter posted to

Jacqueline's Potrero Hill home. That fall, he attended a remedial education program in order to complete his high school equivalency and collect a diploma. It was his last and only choice in terms of a fundamental education. Ironically, he was again tested that summer. His IQ had risen to 142.

After Frank Avion's death, Jacqueline's relationship with her son went from cold to indifferent to shameless disdain. By his last year in school, Byron had been cast off to a windowless room in the basement of his mother's house while she lived in spaciousness upstairs. Jacqueline had also taken to traveling as often as possible, finally delving into the funds that she had so carefully preserved. She simply had no interest in her son, so long as he wasn't causing her problems. Even when the two were together in the same house, on the same floor, Jacqueline did what she could to avoid Byron, and he did likewise. Inexplicably, they stayed together for the rest of his life, one way or the other.

Once again, Byron proved himself to be a chameleon. Despite his obvious dislike for the classroom, he managed to graduate from the Sunview Special School with high honors in 1951. His opportunity to apply for even a moderately prestigious college had long ago vanished in a flurry of flunked classes, yet Byron seemed intent on pursuing a higher education. Given his disastrous high school record and the lack of any emotional ties on the home front, Byron decided to join the military.

Avion wasn't about to offer himself up for any kind of frontline service. That wasn't the point of enlisting. The young man had always been intrigued with his father's Army escapades, even though the Army itself was not to his liking. The Army had provided Frank Avion with a good education. He had worked on interesting projects throughout his military career. He had told his son what he could about intelligence work and, in particular, code breaking. These were memories that Byron truly treasured, and he decided to follow in Frank's footsteps, with one variation on the theme — he would join the Navy and see the world.

In the fall of 1951, Byron enlisted. He contracted with the Navy recruiter for a six-year stint so he could receive a full college education, special training in ciphers and codes, and relative assurance that he would be based somewhere far away from hotspots like Korea. On the day of his enlistment, Jacqueline was traveling in England and didn't receive word of his departure until she returned, three months later.

Unlike that of his father, Byron's military career was short-lived and frustrating for all concerned. The young man could never get his weight under control; he could not abide by the discipline, orderliness, and routine fundamental to military life. Worst of all, Byron found himself completely isolated from his comrades. He was the constant brunt of barracks jokes, generally centered on his physical deficiencies. It made his time at St. Augustus look like a picnic.

Somehow, Byron managed to squeak his way through basic training and was even enrolled in a special school in Washington to study codes and ciphers. But a year later, after barely graduating from code school, he was abruptly offered the back door. The military machine had simply choked on trying to make a soldier and gentleman out of Byron Avion. He could either quit the service without the benefit of an honorable discharge or allow the system to take its course with him, which almost certainly would have sent him into a vastly different kind of military service than he had in mind. Byron didn't think twice. He walked away from the Navy in 1954 and moved in with Jacqueline. He was twenty-one years old.

For the next six years, Avion moved up and down the coast of California, living in a series of towns and cities, including Los Angeles, San Luis Rey, and Riverside. He worked at a variety of odd jobs, usually as a mechanic. Avion had some enviable skills with his hands and a natural understanding of mechanical devices, which served him well in hard economic times. He also continued to work on his education, although his interests had changed considerably from ciphers and codes. Now, Byron professed an intense desire to work with young children. He decided that he wanted to teach at the grammar school level. In 1960, he graduated from the California State University system with a bachelor's degree in education.

In the early 1960s, Avion settled in the San Francisco Bay Area, staying mostly in Jacqueline's house, although he traveled frequently. During these years, he made repeated attempts to get his state teaching credential. He also applied for a variety of jobs at a number of different elementary schools. But Avion was never able to attain either his teaching credential or a teaching job. Instead, he fell back on his lifelong pattern: working at a variety of part-time jobs and retreating to his mother's house when the money ran out.

Toward the end of the 1960s, he moved several times between Riverside and the San Francisco Bay Area, usually in search of a different job. In the years since high school, Avion had always lived alone; he had no significant relationships with a lover, and he had no close friends. He seemed to live the life of an isolated, perpetual student, who survived on low-level jobs and had no obvious plans for his life. Avion was never able to settle in one place, yet he always managed to sustain himself by his wits, which were considerable.

By the end of 1968, Avion was back in San Francisco, once again living with his mother and working part-time in a meaningless, low-paying job. In early 1969, he was fired from his position as a small-motor mechanic in a Mission District assembly plant. It was around this time that he was arrested for disturbing the peace — his only official run-in with the law at that point.

Regardless of the fact that this was a minor infraction, it was a telling incident, at least from Mick Millian's perspective.

Avion was driving through Napa County on a Saturday in the spring of 1969 when he stopped at a roadside restaurant for a break. After finishing a late breakfast at the counter, he left the restaurant and headed toward his car, which was parked in back of the facility. On his way, he noticed a girl of thirteen, sitting in the passenger's seat of an old green pickup truck. She had the window rolled down and was staring at the other cars in the lot, her head resting on the palm of her hand. As Avion strolled to his car, their eyes met, and the girl offered him a shy smile. She was dark-haired, petite, pretty, and mature for her age.

Avion went directly to the passenger's side of the truck and began talking to the girl. For several moments, they exchanged innocuous pleasantries. Then, without explanation, he suddenly reached through the open window and began to stroke the girl's long, ebony hair. Frightened, she jumped back and yelped in surprise. Her father walked around the corner from the front of the restaurant just in time to see a large, burly stranger leaning through the window with his hand on his daughter's head.

The girl's father raced to the front of the truck, yelling and waving his arms. Avion whirled around and saw the stranger rushing at him with clenched fists. In a quick series of moves that belied his considerable bulk, Avion stepped aside and drove his right fist into the man's face, knocking him to the ground and sending him into a semi-conscious stupor.

The girl in the pickup truck screamed at the sight of her father lying on the ground. Three other restaurant patrons appeared in the parking lot and quickly moved toward the pickup. Wisely, Avion made no other moves, nor did he flee the scene. He simply stepped away from the vehicle and stood there silently, surveying what he had done with a tight, taunting smile.

Within moments of the altercation, a Napa Police Department patrol car arrived on the scene. The girl's father recovered quickly enough and was able to get to his feet, but he was in no mood to continue the battle. His daughter was still frantic and frightened by the sight of blood on her father's face, running freely from a broken nose. One of the arriving officers had helped him to the edge of the sidewalk bordering the parking lot, where he sat holding a handkerchief to his face.

The two officers took statements from the father, his daughter, and Avion, along with two of the three patrons who had witnessed some portion of the incident. The girl's father refused to press charges against his assailant and wanted nothing more than to be away from that restaurant and on his way home. He also refused any kind of medical treatment. Fortunately for Avion, this left the Napa PD with few options. Based on the information they had, which was generally vague, they arrested Avion for disturbing the peace and immediately released him. He ultimately paid a small fine. The details and intent of Avion's unhealthy interaction with the thirteen-year-old could only be inferred from her version of the event, and these were too flimsy to warrant any kind of a formal charge. However, Avion's motive must have been clear enough to the young victim and her father. Perhaps that is why he chose not to file charges.

Through the rest of 1969 and into 1970, Avion lived in his mother's house, making occasional trips to Southern California. He had no visible means of support until mid-year, when he landed a part-time job in the City in a downtown department store. Later that year, he enrolled in classes at Santa Rosa Junior College and began traveling up and down Highway 101 from San Francisco to the campus. His curriculum included a variety of first- and second-year math and science courses. It was during this time that he learned about a janitorial job at the Del Bridge Elementary School in Santa Rosa. By early 1971, he was working at the school two nights a week, mostly on an irregular basis. That job would later become more stable, with longer and more consistent hours.

In early 1971, Avion could claim two legal residences. His primary address was still with his mother in the Potrero Hill District of San Francisco. However, he had also rented a cheap apartment near the SRJC campus. By this time, Avion was beginning to establish a permanent presence in the Santa Rosa area that would last for the rest of his life.

Not long after Avion rented the Santa Rosa apartment, his cousin, Sally Ventable, made the call to Inspector Sam Lionell that would drag him into the heart of the Zodiac case, at least for a few months. At the time of Lionell's interest, Avion still held a job as a stockman in San Francisco, the janitorial position at Del Bridge, and was attending classes at the SRJC most mornings. His schedule was becoming impossible to balance, so Avion quit his job in the City and began to spend more time in Santa Rosa. This change in lifestyle had an unexpected impact on Jacqueline Avion.

By her own admission, Jacqueline was never close to her son. She really had little use for him. Still, she would always harbor him during the hard times, slip him sufficient money to keep him in relative comfort, and provide sanctuary through the years when he seemed unable to settle in one place. Now that Byron had all but moved permanently to Santa Rosa, Jacqueline once again rewrote her life script. She sold her home in the City and moved to Santa Rosa, buying the former Pinelli house on Callihan Creek Road.

Around the same time that Jacqueline was making her inexplicable move north, Sam Lionell, Manny Bruin, and Mick Millian had gathered the legal resources they needed to search Avion's apartment near the SRJC campus. When Avion quit his job at the Del Bridge Elementary School, vacated his apartment, and disappeared from his classes at the junior college in late 1972, he was already looking like a strong suspect in what came to be known as the Highway 101 Murders.

But by the early days of 1973, Manny Bruin had no idea what had happened to Avion. The detective had a series of murders to solve, a potential suspect that could not be found, and almost no forensic evidence of value to the investigation. He needed a good deal of help and luck to make something happen in the case, but he had no idea where to look for it.

Someone Always Remembers

Lynn Howard's remains were discovered on July 4, 1973 by a group of three teenage boys who pulled their pickup truck to the shoulder of a road east of town to fix a flat. While two of the boys worked on the tire, their friend idled away the time by poking around the rim of a shallow culvert below the road. There, he thought he spotted something odd — something that looked like a discarded, disfigured storefront manikin, so he returned to tell his friends. When the curious teenagers scrambled down the hillside to get a closer look, they realized that they had stumbled upon the decaying corpse of a young, nude woman with dark hair. The victim was lying on her side, partially covered in the underbrush, less than a hundred feet from the spot where the remains of Mary Spooner and Elaine Calley were found the previous December. What the frightened boys had come across was the body of Lynn Howard, who had disappeared five months earlier while hitchhiking along Highway 101.

It took several days for Cynthia Turgell to make a positive identification of the remains, and nearly two weeks to determine a cause of death. The dumpsite held no clues as to Lynn Howard's fate, when she had died, or the identity of her killer. The decaying corpse showed no obvious signs of trauma or evidence of bindings.

Because of the location of the dumpsite, both Bruin and Millian were reasonably certain that Howard was the latest victim of the Highway 101 Murderer. They couldn't be absolutely sure, however, without much more forensic evidence. Turgell's findings did not help to clarify matters.

The killer's previous victims had been attacked physically, strangled, sometimes molested, and usually tied and beaten. There had always been strong evidence of intense personal contact between the killer and his victims. Lynn Howard had apparently suffered a much different fate. From what Turgell could determine, Howard had been given, or somehow ingested, a massive dose of strychnine. She had suffered no other physical or sexual abuse — at least none that Turgell could identify from the remains. She had not been bound like the others, nor had she apparently been beaten. Probably after her death, Howard's clothes and jewelry had been removed before her body was dumped. The killer had then made an attempt to cover the young woman with underbrush, but had not completely succeeded. From the look of the dumpsite, it appeared that he had not been as careful with Lynn's body as he had been with Mary and Elaine. Perhaps the killer had been rushed or interrupted.

The use of poison seemed completely out of character. It led to the uncomfortable possibility that Lynn may not have been killed by the same fugitive that Bruin and Millian were hunting. Was it possible that there were *two* killers on the loose? If that was true, it was an amazing coincidence that the murderer would have selected the same location to dump Howard's body where investigators had earlier found Mary and Elaine's. Had this second killer been influenced by press reports of the Highway 101 Murderer?

Death by strychnine poisoning is a horrible fate. Strychnine is a natural toxin used against rodents and as a fungicide, and is readily available to the public, especially in rural communities. This was certainly the case in the 1970s in Santa Rosa, at a time when toxic substances such as strychnine were less regulated than they are today. Once strychnine is ingested, the poison begins to attack the body's central nervous system within as little as ten minutes, and certainly within a half-hour. It has a bitter taste that is difficult to disguise in any significant quantity, but not much of the poison is needed to be fatal — just 15 to 30 milligrams. Once absorbed, it causes severe, uncontrollable, and exceptionally painful convulsions. In a short period of time, without extreme medical intervention, these convulsions will cause the breathing to stop. Lynn Howard was a slight girl, just over a hundred pounds, so it would not have taken much of the poison to kill her. Her death was surely excruciating.

The fact that Lynn died from strychnine poisoning raised a wealth of new and perplexing issues. Had the victim known her attacker? Had she trusted him sufficiently to ingest the poison unknowingly? Had she been forced to take it? It seemed unlikely that Lynn's killer would have been driving up and down the freeway with some kind of a drink spiked with strychnine, just waiting for his next victim. Did this mean that he took Howard somewhere else before he killed her — to a location where he could prepare and administer the poison? Did he win her trust in some way, drive her to a secure location, and then give her strychnine?

Did the murderer stalk Lynn for some time before he attacked her? If so, could the detectives find a likely suspect in her past — a spurned lover? Was this the work of a serial killer who struck at random or someone who had specifically targeted the victim in an act of retribution? If Lynn's murder was a crime of retribution, the SCCID was unable to nail down any individual who expressed dislike for the young woman. The attack seemed to lack an obvious personal motive, which was certainly in keeping with what Bruin and Millian had come to know about their fugitive serial killer.

Lynn Howard's bizarre and hideous death gave Bruin's investigation an unwelcome dimension that took on a life of its own: whether or not the SCCID was dealing with a single killer or two. Her murder inspired a barrage of questions and criticisms from the media and the public, much of it out of left field, threatening to put the SCCID investigation back months. Bruin was frantic about this radical change in the course of his case and the added pressure that it caused. He grew increasingly frustrated, and his foul mood was beginning to wear on those close to him. Unfortunately, neither Turgell nor Millian could do anything to ease his mind; they had questions of their own that couldn't be answered.

The Santa Rosa *Journal* was quick in attributing Lynn Howard's murder to the Highway 101 Murderer, despite Manny's public assurances that the SCCID wasn't ruling out other possibilities. On several occasions Manny pointed out that this could well have been a crime of passion or an act of retribution by someone close to the victim. Nonetheless, the *Journal* stuck to its story. The newspaper argued that the dumpsite where her remains were discovered was much more than a coincidental choice. It was a message of some kind — as was the missing clothes, jewelry, and personal effects. Secretly, Manny agreed with them, but was careful to keep that opinion within the walls of the SCCID.

The Santa Rosa newspaper also ran a lengthy retrospective on the Highway 101 Murderer's string of victims, who now numbered six: Spooner, Calley, Alverson, Kantell (by this time, presumed to be a victim, but not yet confirmed), Buono, and Howard. The *Journal* pointed out that the series of murders had started in February 1972 and now, more than a year later, the SCCID was still unusually quiet about developments and had given no indication that a suspect had been named. Although the SCCID made occasional public announcements that they were convinced there were no other victims of the fugitive killer and that the investigation was proceeding normally, the *Journal* was openly dubious. The paper suggested that there might be many bodies hidden or buried in the vast areas of undeveloped land that surrounded Santa Rosa. With the large number of teenage girls who ran away from home each year, the newspaper argued that no one could be sure how many of them had fallen victim to the killer.

Although the *Journal's* retrospective was predictably sensational, and more than a little annoying to the SCCID, it scored heavily with the public as it hammered home the uncertainties and apparent lack of progress in the investigation, as well as the specter of a second killer raised by Howard's poisoning.

None of this went down well with Manny Bruin. He was besieged with worried calls from the public, a constant ringing in his ears from the local politicos, officials, bosses, and political wannabes, and a flood of new tips, all of which had to be checked out as thoroughly as possible. As he expected, none of them proved to be of any value; but they did have the same untoward effect as the ceaseless phone calls — dragging out the investigation even further. What Bruin wanted most was to take back the investigation from the realm of public scrutiny and make some *real* headway. But first came the telephone, the telephone, and then the telephone.

By the end of that summer, the case had evolved into the most notorious criminal event in Santa Rosa's history, and it was beginning to whittle away at the public's trust in the SCCID. Moreover, it had some eerie, disturbing parallels to the Zodiac investigation that was still proceeding in the San Francisco Bay Area. The last thing Bruin wanted was for his case to become swallowed up in the media feeding frenzy and public paranoia that had crippled Sam Lionell's Zodiac investigation.

Soon after the *Journal* printed its retrospective, Bruin held a series of public press conferences to make sure that the SCCID version of the story received equal time with the local population. Unfortunately, he had little to offer, which only served to substantiate the confusion and concern that the *Journal* had already reported. Now, everyone in town was aware of the Highway 101 Murderer and the SCCID's apparent inability to do anything about it.

December 1973
Terry Calan

One year to the day on which Mary Calley and Elaine Spooner's remains were discovered, Terry Calan vanished while hitchhiking north on Highway 101. Calan was 21 years old but looked five years younger. She was lean, petite, dark-haired and quick with a smile. Her nickname, "Pixie," was a perfect reflection of the image she conveyed to those around her. Calan was also the mother of a two-year old boy, who lived with her parents in Eureka. On the day of her disappearance, Terry was heading north to her family home to spend the holidays with her son, two brothers, and her parents.

Terry's father reported his daughter's disappearance to the Eureka Police Department on Christmas Eve. The Calans had expected Terry to arrive two or three days earlier, but waited to file the report because Terry often ran late, sometimes by several days. The Eureka PD made a preliminary investigation, but soon decided it was just another runaway case, despite the fact that Terry had been living on her own since she was seventeen. A copy of Calan's missing persons report made its way to Mick Millian's desk ten days later — the same day that a local rancher reported the discovery of a partially nude body that had been dumped along a creek on his property. It was Terry Calan.

If there had been endless speculation about who had murdered Lynn Howard the previous summer, there was none about Terry Calan's killer. Terry had been tied around her wrists and ankles with white nylon rope. She had been brutally beaten, sexually molested, and thrown down the creek bed in an area close to where the body of Leslie Buono had been discovered in December 1972. And the location was less than a mile from where Cathy Alverson had been dumped in April of that year.

Calan's murder had all the unmistakable earmarks of the fugitive serial killer, including the absence of personal effects and jewelry on the body. And, like all the other crime scenes, it offered next to nothing in the way of forensic evidence.

With the discovery of Terry Calan's remains, the Santa Rosa *Journal* went into a feeding frenzy that was reminiscent of the San Francisco *Chronicle*'s reaction to the Zodiac case. In January and February, the newspaper ran seven articles that dealt with the Highway 101 Murders in detail, including timelines, backgrounds of the victims, and all the details that they had gathered about the crimes and the dumpsites. Bruin was furious.

In every intensive, high-profile criminal investigation, law enforcement personnel try to hold back one or more pieces of crucial information or evidence that they can later use to link a suspect with the crimes. Often, this is a key piece of forensic evidence. Now, in this case, the SCCID had nothing to hold back. Virtually everything that was known about the case had appeared in the *Journal*, including information about the pieces of white nylon rope that had been found at most of the dumpsites. The only bit of information that had escaped the attention of the local media was the name of Mick Millian's favorite suspect, Byron Avion. Bruin was amazed and grateful that this had somehow escaped the *Journal's* attention. Had Avion's name appeared in the pages of the local newspaper, Bruin was certain that Millian, himself, and the SCCID would all be on the losing end of a big, fat, ugly lawsuit. Thankfully, that didn't happen.

At the height of the fury over Terry Calan's murder, several relatives of the victims demanded to meet with Bruin and Millian about the status of the investigation. They were understandably angry and frustrated that the killing was continuing, and they wanted some definitive answers. Bruin was quick to agree to a private meeting and spent over seven hours with three-dozen participants in an SCCID conference room. It was a wrenching, painful day for everyone involved and, in the end, it did little to shed new light on the investigation. Still, it mattered deeply to the families, and Bruin promised that he would meet with them anytime they wanted in order to keep them informed on the progress of the case. The next day, the *Journal* reported favorably on Bruin's efforts, quoting at length from some of the positive remarks made by members of the victims' families. This was the first bit of good press for the SCCID in months and it had the effect of picking up morale around the office. The meeting did, however, have one conspicuous absentee: Bill Calley. When Bruin asked Millian why Calley had not come, Mick was uncharacteristically vague and claimed that he didn't know. Manny didn't buy his partner's explanation, but he didn't press the issue, and soon forgot all about it.

That same month, Bruin received a phone call from Sam Lionell — his first contact with the SFPD inspector in months. The SFPD had come into possession of a letter that Zodiac had written to the San Francisco *Chronicle* a few weeks earlier and

Lionell wanted to check on the whereabouts of Byron Avion. It seemed that Avion was still swimming around on Lionell's suspect list.

This was the first missive from Zodiac since March 1971, and Lionell was stunned at its contents. Zodiac had written to express his fondness for the blockbuster movie, *The Exorcist*, which was playing in theaters across the country. Unlike Zodiac's previous letters, this one contained no threats, no attempts at intimidation, and no claims of additional victims. The style of the letter was completely uncharacteristic. It did not open with the killer's traditional greeting, "This is the Zodiac speaking," nor did the writer affix his special cross-hair symbol. In effect, no casual observer would have guessed that the Zodiac had written it. However, Lionell had the document examined by experts in Sacramento who concluded that the handwriting matched that of known Zodiac letters. Why the serial killer had written at this particular time, and why he had suddenly taken on the role of movie critic, was something that Lionell didn't understand and couldn't explain. Perhaps his friend at the SCCID could shed some light?

Bruin assured Lionell that he was still hot on the trail of Byron Avion, although he had no idea where to pick up the search. As far as he knew, Avion had nothing to do with the latest letter or any of the other Zodiac letters. On the other hand, could Lionell be of any help to the SCCID in tracking Avion down? No, sorry. Was

Lionell sure that Zodiac had written that last letter? Well, yes, pretty sure. Was Avion still a suspect in the Zodiac investigation? Well, maybe...

By the end of the call, Manny was left shaking his head. If there was any connection between Avion and Zodiac, he couldn't see it. The whole conversation left him with the impression that Sam Lionell was way short on leads and getting desperate — a situation with which Manny Bruin could identify.

In March, Bruin was unexpectedly given a three-man team of investigators from the SRPD to help support the hitchhiker murder investigation. The team's role was to re-examine each of the crimes in detail, re-investigate the background of each of the victims, re-interview everyone who had been involved in the case, and try to develop a fresh list of suspects. For the duration of the assignment, they would report to Bruin on their progress and be involved in every aspect of the SCCID investigation. Manny was happy for the help, but a bit suspicious of the timing and purpose. The three law enforcement agencies in the area, the Sheriff's Office, the SRPD, and the SCCID, were each receiving their fair share of heat from the press, the local politicians, and the public. Throwing additional investigators at the case was one way to ease some of this pressure. But Bruin also understood that this kind of strategy often led to interdepartmental snooping and battles, hoarding of potential clues, and, worst of all, a kind of public rivalry that could set the investigation back even further.

Publicly, Bruin accepted the help with a smile, participating enthusiastically in the press fanfare that the gift was intended to generate. Privately, he did more listening than talking with the SRPD team. It became obvious that they were going over old ground and doing it with a relish that Manny found frustrating and annoying. Bruin didn't like the implication that the SCCID may have missed something important, but he couldn't deny the possibility, at least publicly. So, he was polite and cooperative, but little more. To his surprise, Millian ignored the SRPD team, almost without exception. Bruin had expected his partner to be angry with the SRPD's role, and vocal about their tactics, but Mick showed little interest in the subject. He just went about his business, intent on working the Avion angle in his own way. He kept Bruin informed about his lack of progress and rarely bothered to sit in on the joint meetings with the SRPD team and his partner. He was usually able to produce some pressing reason why he needed to be elsewhere.

In June, Bruin received another call from Sam Lionell. Zodiac had written a second letter to the *Chronicle*. This time, the killer was complaining about the sensationalism of violence that he had witnessed in a movie he had recently attended. Once again, the letter gave no overt indication that it had been written by Zodiac, but the handwriting had been confirmed in Sacramento. Had Manny heard anything from Byron Avion lately? Did he know Avion's whereabouts? No, no, no! It was another desperate, frustrating conversation between two investigators who were falling further and further behind their respective suspects.

Unknown to Manny Bruin, Byron Avion was moving closer to the surface, and Bill Calley was the driving force.

July 1974
Bill, Mick, and Jacqueline

In Washington, Watergate Special Prosecutor Jaworski had forced Richard Nixon to turn over 64 secret tape recordings of White House conversations that would unequivocally implicate the President in a massive cover-up. It was the beginning of the end for Nixon, who would resign a month later, on August 9. It was clear that the man who held the highest post in our country had not kept faith with the American public. Out west in Santa Rosa, Bill Calley had kept the ultimate faith. He had been an icon of discretion and a bastion of trust. Bill Calley and Mick Millian had always trusted each other, especially when it came to Byron Avion.

From Mick's point of view, there were two obvious reasons to involve his old friend in the Highway 101 Murderer case. Bill wanted to be a part of the solution — a part of the resolution — to his daughter's brutal murder. In fact, he wanted nothing more from life than this. Mick's other reason was more pragmatic but no less important: Avion had been more successful in keeping the pressure on Millian than the other way around. Mick's intensity, his passion to solve these crimes, had nearly been his undoing.

Manny had made it all very clear. Mick could stay with the investigation, but he had better stay out of Avion's face, at least until they had something solid. It was a tight leash — but no one could leash Bill Calley. He was a private citizen and a figure who generated a good deal of sympathy, especially inside the SCCID and the court system where he worked. Bill could do many things that his friend, Mick, could not, including keeping an eye on Avion. Unfortunately, Avion had made the first move and vanished. Now, it didn't seem to matter what the SCCID did, they couldn't find his trail. What the SCCID didn't know was that Millian had already put a plan in place to solve this problem.

The deal that had been struck between Bill Calley and Mick Millian started off simply enough. He would help Mick keep an eye on the suspect and report back on anything that he observed. It would be Bill and Mick's secret, safe from Bruin or anyone else, including the rest of the Calley family. If anything came to fruition, they would go straight to Manny, make up some kind of cover story, and put the evidence on the table.

The arrangement had been established early on, before the discovery of Mary and Elaine's remains. After Paul Buchette recalled the battered green VW in front of the ice skating rink where the girls were last seen, Mick began to piece things together. In truth, he had already jumped to a monumental conclusion about

Byron Avion. As matters developed over the next year and a half — as more girls and women died — Millian's assumption began to look increasingly viable, even to his ever-skeptical boss. The problem with Millian's pet theory was one of legalities and logistics. There was no pragmatic reason to treat Avion as a suspect, and the SCCID had better stay out of his face, until they had some legal reason to get into his face.

Enter Bill Calley — Mick's secret weapon. Bill could go where Mick could not. He could observe, ask discreet questions of bystanders and neighbors, search court records with ease, and do much more, all without leaving a trace. It was a deal struck on the basis of a long friendship and on Mick's assumption that Bill's activities would be minimal and risk-free. But Bill saw a much more active role for himself. He just didn't bother to tell Millian.

After Avion vacated his apartment, quit his job, and disappeared from his SRJC classes, Calley committed himself to finding him. Like his ethereal adversary, Bill knew the Santa Rosa area inside and out. Calley examined all the options, asking himself where Avion would go and why. Bill spent hundreds of hours studying the information that Millian had given him on Avion's background. He became intimately familiar with the man, his habits, his lifestyle, and his reasoning. He knew that Avion had a second residence, or at least a resting place, somewhere in the area. Calley guessed that this was where Avion headed when he left his apartment near the junior college. This, he decided, would become his mission: to find that residence — to find out where Avion was staying — and report back to Mick.

Calley focused on the rural areas west of Santa Rosa. This part of Sonoma County is sparsely populated and very large. It encompasses hundreds of square miles of rolling hills and thick redwood forests that stretch to the Pacific Ocean. The land is punctuated by countless streams, two major rivers, and riddled with tiny homes nestled in the forests. Once a huge logging domain, the terrain is rife with uncharted backcountry dirt roads that meander among the hills. In the 1970s, it was the perfect place for someone who craved isolation. The magnitude and remoteness of the terrain eventually made Calley's job impossible, no matter how tirelessly he pursued it.

Bill would spend days in the Russian River area, searching the logging roads and trails for the one real clue that he had — a white sedan. He soon became known to the townsfolk in Guerneville, Rio Nido, and Cazadero as an avid fisherman and solo camper. In his quiet, unassuming way, Bill gained the trust of several shopkeepers in these small towns and got to know the comings and goings of the locals. Gradually, imperceptibly, he would draw his conversations with the townsfolk closer to his ultimate target, the white sedan, and to the large man who loved his isolation. But in the end, it all came to nothing. If Byron Avion had retreated to the hills and forests west of Santa Rosa, he had done an excellent job of losing himself.

Over time, Calley finally realized the enormity of his search. He came to the reluctant conclusion that if his efforts ever proved fruitful, it would be sheer luck.

But Calley had one card left to play. He and Mick had talked about the possibility of Bill getting to know Jacqueline Avion — to learn what she knew, perhaps to learn something about her son's whereabouts. Calley was cool on the idea. He found the thought of dealing with the mother of the man who may have murdered his daughter unbearable. But even Bill understood why he was the right man for the job. There was no possibility of Millian approaching Jacqueline Avion. She was just as off-limits as Avion himself.

When Bill's search failed, Mick and his friend were out of options, and the SCCID itself seemed paralyzed. The Jacqueline Avion alternative suddenly became more appealing. In the summer following the discovery of Terry Calan's remains, the friends decided it was time to act. Calley would call on Jacqueline Avion at her home. Mick would carefully brief him on how to handle the situation, how to get the most out of what was sure to be a short, ugly, and testy encounter. If she had something — anything at all — he would try to finesse it out of her and bring it straight back to Millian. If that didn't work, well, they were stuck.

Mid-morning on the following Saturday, Bill Calley rapped on the front door at 1654 Callihan Creek Road. From the outside, the house seemed unoccupied, as it always did. The deep blue curtains were tightly drawn, despite the warm, inviting brightness of the morning. For some time, Calley listened intently, barely breathing, hoping to catch some sound of life from beyond the door.

He rapped again with the back of his right hand, this time with a steady, insistent rhythm that would be difficult to ignore. Once again, he waited, standing quiet and still. He heard a distant shuffling of feet that seemed to move toward the door. Finally, it swung open, just wide enough to permit the aging woman to squeeze her narrow face around its corner. She squinted her eyes in the daylight as she tried to focus on the man who had been knocking. Calley decided to take the initiative, just the way Mick had briefed him.

"Mrs. Avion?" He spoke in a polite tone, being careful not to sound like a salesman.

She cleared her throat and shook her head. "I'm not interested," she announced in a stern, deep voice.

"No, Mrs. Avion, I'm not selling anything. I'm here on a personal matter and I won't take much of your time. It's very important ma'am." He tried to look as innocent as possible.

Jacqueline surveyed the man on her doorstep. She reached across the top of her head and dragged her rimless glasses down over her sharp nose. She focused on Bill Calley's face. After several seconds, he could see her narrow eyes begin to widen and soften. Something had registered.

"I know who you are," she whispered in a slow, methodical tone. "You're Elaine Calley's father, aren't you?"

Calley was stunned. How could she possibly know him? He searched his memory, but could not recall a meeting. His mind raced back to the moment at hand. What was he going to do now? What could he say? All of Mick's careful advice, all the scenarios that they had worked out, it all vanished with her simple, leveling statement.

Without speaking, Bill reached into the pocket of his tweed sport jacket and withdrew a small color photograph with frayed edges. It was something he always kept with him. He pushed it toward the woman in the doorway.

Jacqueline dropped her head and examined the photo for several seconds through a tangle of shoulder-length gray curls. When she lifted her head again, her eyes were wet. Their color had changed from a cold blue to almost green.

"I was at the service, Mr. Calley. I was there... at Christmas time," she mumbled, staring at him in a vague, unfocussed way.

Calley still couldn't think of anything to say so he rolled his head up and down in a motion of understanding. His stomach was rocketing out of control. The trembling of his hands made the photograph of Elaine and Mary in front of the Calley's Christmas tree shake. He pulled the photo back and put it carefully into his pocket. He stood frozen on her doorstep. For a moment, she did the same.

"I think you had better come in, Mr. Calley," she said. She tugged at the door until it was fully open stepping aside for her guest to pass. But Bill remained motionless, just staring at her. Jacqueline was wearing a deep purple, single-piece dress that seemed more appropriate for a dinner date than a morning around the house. On her feet were black, flat loafers that couldn't have been more poorly matched to her dress if a blind woman had selected them. Above the rim of the loafers, she had rolled down her white socks several times, just to ankle level. Her hair was thick, curly, and surrounded her face like armor.

"I think you'd better come in," she repeated, this time with a gentle authority. "I'm glad you came, Mr. Calley..." He caught the first hint of a smile. It was tight and thin, just like her son's.

Jacqueline walked away from the door and shuffled into the front room, leaving Bill waiting outside, uncertain what to do. He stood there for a while longer, debating his next step. This was the moment that he had waited for — a chance to get closer to Avion. He shook his arms and hands to get the blood flowing. The woman he had assumed would be a formidable and defensive adversary had transformed herself into something unexpected. It was time for the truth, regardless of the damage that it might cause.

Calley stepped into the darkened, unfamiliar hallway. He closed the heavy door behind him and rubbed his eyes to help focus. The room was silent, cool, and much too still for his liking.

Bill could see Jacqueline hovering over a heavy mahogany table at the far wall of the living room. She draped her thin hand across the top of an ornately framed photograph in the center of the table, clearly the most important of the dozens of trinkets and knickknacks that were on display there. In the murkiness of the living room, she was partly silhouetted by the few rays of tawny light that found their way through the thick curtains. He stood between the hallway and the living room, staring at her outline, watching her intently.

"Mr. Calley, I have a photograph that you should see." She spoke in a hoarse whisper, without turning in his direction.

Bill crossed the nearly black hardwood floor that separated the hallway from the living room. As he entered the room and reached the thick, richly patterned rug, he picked up his pace until he stood directly behind Jacqueline. She turned slowly to face him. Her eyes were even larger than before, the pupils dilated in the darkness. A narrow rivulet of tears had rolled across her rouged checks and down the side of her jaw, dragging minute fragments of eye shadow. She pulled the framed photograph from the table and offered it to her guest.

Calley grasped the side of the heavy metal frame and tried to focus on the two figures looking back at him. Jacqueline brushed past him and walked to the nearest window, which faced the front of the house. She drew back the curtains and flooded the room with light. As the brightness raced across the face of the photograph, Calley gasped and took a step backward.

Staring back at him was the image of two young girls, probably around twelve or thirteen years old. Both were wrapped in frilly white dresses, arm in arm, beaming back at the camera. Behind them was what appeared to be a church, its wide, thick wooden door flung open. The photo looked old — very old. But what had taken Bill aback was the girl on the left. Although the snapshot wasn't much more than a grainy black-and-white image, the girl on the left looked like his daughter, Elaine. In fact, she could have been Elaine's twin. She had Elaine's broad, oversized smile, her light hair, petite build, and flowing, delicate fingers. Bill's hands began to shake, then his chest, and finally his legs. He felt himself falling away from the photograph, from the room. Then he felt a determined tug on his left arm. It was Jacqueline Avion.

She guided him to the long couch under the window, where he gave himself up to a noisy sitting-fall into the cushions. The framed photograph slid onto his lap. He closed his eyes and began to cry, softly at first, then with a series of shudders that gripped his body. Jacqueline sat next to him and said nothing. After a moment, she began to stroke his left forearm with her hand, almost imperceptibly, then with determination and concern.

It took several moments for Calley to regain control. He swallowed noisily and opened his eyes, blinking hard against the salty wetness. She was still sitting next to him, alternately staring at his face, then at the photograph in his lap. She took her hand from his arm and raised it to chest level. With a bent finger, she poked at the photograph in his lap.

"That was me, Mr. Calley. I'm the one on the left. It was taken when I was thirteen years old, in Santa Barbara. The girl on the right, Marianne, was my best friend. A few months after that picture was taken, Marianne was murdered. When I read about your daughter's murder — when I saw all the photographs in the paper — I had to come to the service. You can see why."

She sighed and turned away, perching on the edge of the couch and staring across the living room. She began to fiddle with the edge of her dress, making folds in it and sighing. He could sense that she was fighting back tears.

Bill pulled the photograph close again and studied the image. It was true. The resemblance was uncanny, frightening. It was an indescribable, wrenching experience.

A minute later, Jacqueline slid from the couch, stood in the center of the room, then turned to face her guest. She was breathing normally now. Her face was dry, and her posture seemed more determined, more confident.

"I'm going to make some tea, Mr. Calley. Would you like some?"

He nodded and rose from the couch, unsure about what he should do.

"No, no," she said, waving her hand. "You wait here, Mr. Calley. It will take me a few moments. I'll be back with the tea and some other things for you."

She shuffled away, toward the hallway, but another thought crossed her mind. She turned quickly, bending slightly at the hips as if to emphasize what she had to say.

"I think I know why you're here, Mr. Calley. Let me assure you... Well... I want to help you if I can. It's time that I did something right for a change, and maybe this is my chance."

Before her guest could reply, Jacqueline had disappeared, down the hallway, into the darkness. From the couch, Bill heard the sound of an old wooden door being pulled open, its ill-fitting outline scraping at the frame. Then he heard the sound of shuffling feet in flat shoes moving slowly down wooden steps, fading into the silence. Then, nothing.

Boxes and Secrets

Ten minutes passed before Bill Calley heard his hostess shuffling back up the wooden stairs. It had seemed like hours. When she finally entered the room, Jacqueline was carrying a brown cardboard box that had been neatly tied with white nylon rope. Her thin arms were wrapped snugly around its perimeter, her hands clasped together at its front. Bill snapped to his feet and stepped toward her.

"Can I help you with that?" he offered.

"Thank you, Mr. Calley, it *is* a bit heavy for me." She struggled to hand the box to her guest.

As he grasped the box, Calley could feel several objects shuffle around inside. It felt like a few stacks of paper, or books, rubbing against cardboard. It was lighter than he had expected from Jacqueline's efforts. There were no markings on any of the surfaces. The outside of the box felt dry to the touch, but the fiber of the cardboard gave off a musty, damp odor. The aroma drew his thoughts to the room downstairs, to the possibility that there were other boxes down there, with other secrets. He wondered why his hostess had selected this one.

"Please, put it on the coffee table, there," she instructed, gesturing toward the low mahogany table in front of the couch. "That would be fine, Mr. Calley, over there."

He nodded, turned, and gently set the box on the table.

"Good, thanks," she said, still in a serious tone. "I'll get that tea now and be right back. You can go ahead and look inside the box if you like, or you can wait for me to come back if that would make you more comfortable. These are some of my son's personal effects. You may want to look at them. However, I must warn you that you won't like some of what you see, so please don't go in there if you'd rather not."

Without further explanation, she abruptly turned and left the room, heading down the hallway to the kitchen at the back of the house.

Calley sat on the edge of the couch and stared at the box. It was just like the cardboard boxes that had driven Mick Millian crazy with curiosity. The detective had seen Byron Avion moving similar boxes in and out of his apartment near the SRJC campus, and in and out of several of his vehicles. Each box looked the same — plain, brown cardboard, about two feet square, carefully tied with white nylon rope knotted at the top. Millian was convinced that they contained information that Avion would never want anyone to know. He was sure that somewhere, in one of those boxes, was everything that the SCCID would need to prove that Avion was a killer.

Millian had made a point to impress his friend with how closely Avion guarded these boxes. Obviously, he had been wrong, at least as far as Avion's mother was concerned. Now, Calley had the chance that Millian had so desperately wanted — an opportunity to look inside one of Avion's boxes. It seemed too good to be true; but it was also frightening.

Unconsciously, Bill shook his head, trying to fight off the intense confusion of the last few moments. Everything was moving too quickly. Nothing had gone as he and Mick had planned it. Jacqueline Avion was not at all what he had expected. Now, she was apparently ready to share personal information about her son with a man whom she didn't know. None of this made sense to Bill — except for the old photograph of Mrs. Avion and her best friend.

It was obvious to Calley that Jacqueline had been profoundly moved by Elaine's death. She had apparently identified herself with Elaine in some bizarre but deeply moving way — identified herself with a girl two generations removed, who could have easily passed for her identical twin at the age of twelve. Like Elaine, Jacqueline had lost her best friend to a killer, strengthening the bond between the events of the past and the present. All of this must have been working away at Jacqueline's soul ever since she had learned of Elaine Calley's murder and saw the girl's photograph in the *Journal*.

In one aspect, all of this made sense: the inestimable shock of senseless murder that had cut its way through his life and hers. He could understand the intensity of that pain. But was this enough motivation for what she now offered him? He didn't know, but he wasn't about to waste the moment.

Calley reached out and pulled the coffee table closer to the couch, positioning it and the box so that the prize was directly in front of him. He tugged at one of the loose ends of the bow-tie knot on top of the box and watched the tension of the bindings relax. Slipping his right forefinger under the two, crossed strands, he pulled them away from the cardboard and let them fall to the table. For a moment, Bill stared at the unsealed top, uncertain about delving further. With a deliberate slowness, Bill alternately pulled on each of the four cardboard flaps and folded them against the sides of the box. Then, after taking a breath, he leaned over to look inside.

"Ah... I see you've opened it," Jacqueline announced in a loud voice. She shuffled across the thick carpet in his direction. She was carrying a polished black lacquer tray on which she had arranged a formal tea service. He said nothing, at first. The bolts of crimson across his cheeks said everything.

"Well, not yet... I haven't been inside yet," he answered sheepishly. "To be honest, Mrs. Avion, I'm very confused and not sure if I *want* to look inside there."

Jacqueline set the ornate tray on the edge of the table and took a moment to neatly realign the two china cups that had slid about during their journey. She stood up stiffly, laid her right hand across the small of her back, and stretched, as if the act of carrying the tray had made her ache.

"Yes, Mr. Calley, I understand," she said softly. "Perhaps we should talk a bit first, before you go through the box. Would that be better?" Her voice was gentle and even.

He nodded his agreement but said nothing; his eyes were still fixed on the box, his cheeks still warm to the touch.

Jacqueline moved around the coffee table and slid the open box to the far end, well out of his reach. She positioned the tray in the center of the table where the box had been and sat down on the couch next to him.

"Would you like some tea?" she offered.

"No, ma'am."

"All right, then." She poured herself a cup of over-steeped Earl Gray from an ornate oriental pot with red dragons racing across its fat belly. She poured him one anyway, but left it on the tray.

"I'm sorry, Mrs. Avion," he mumbled, staring across the room. "Maybe it was a bad idea that I came here today."

"Oh, no, I don't think so," she quickly answered. "I'm sure you have a very good reason to be here. I'm sure of that."

She eased herself back on the couch and began to sip her tea. For several moments, neither of them spoke. Calley continued to stare at the box on the table but his mind was far away. He was back in his own home, nearly two years ago, with Elaine. Mary was there. It was Christmas. She was smiling, chattering, happy, and so alive...

"Mr. Calley, do you believe that my son had anything to do with your daughter's death?" she asked softly.

"Yes... well... I don't know... I suppose I do, ma'am."

"I see. Well, I suspected as much. There would be no other reason for you to come and see me, I suppose." Her voice was strangely unemotional. She sipped again on her cup of tea as if she didn't have a care in the world.

"Mrs. Avion, you *must* suspect something also or you wouldn't have offered me this." He pointed at the box with a shaky finger. "You *must* have doubts about your son..."

"Oh, my, yes," she replied. "I have many, many doubts about Byron, Mr. Calley. I have many reasons to doubt him. Some of them are in that box."

Bill slid forward on the couch and perched on the edge of the cushion. He turned to face her. Her expression was still impassive.

"I need to know, Mrs. Avion. I need to know what happened to Elaine and Mary, and the others. I need to have justice for my daughter and I need some peace for myself and my family." His voice was insistent but not angry.

She turned and stared intently into his eyes, so intently that he had to drop his head. Her thin face, high cheekbones, tight, undernourished lips, and thick gray hair cast a formidable image, an image that could easily have frightened a young boy.

"Is it justice or revenge, Mr. Calley? Do you know which you're looking for today?" Her voice was still soft but her words were precise and cutting.

"I hope it's justice," he answered without looking up. "I'm not the kind of man who seeks revenge."

She studied him for a few more seconds, then turned away and slid back into the couch. "No, I don't think you are, Mr. Calley. I have every reason to believe that you're a good man. Yet, you're convinced that my son is a murderer. You know, you're not the first person to believe that, and I suppose you won't be the last." Although she refused to look at him, her voice had become soft and inviting, much less stern than before.

"Did he kill Elaine?" Calley asked after a moment of silence.

"I don't know, Mr. Calley," came the reply.

"*Could* he have killed her?"

"I don't know..." Her voice was barely a whisper.

"Then what's in the box? Why do you want me to see what's in there?" Bill asked.

"It's a part of Byron that he hides from the world, Mr. Calley. It's a part of him that I fear... it's the part of him that you should fear. Maybe it will help answer your questions, maybe not. I don't know..."

Calley shook his head, interrupting her. "I don't understand, ma'am. Why would you want me to see this part of your son? What's the point?"

"Because it may help you. Because I need *your* help, Mr. Calley."

She slipped her empty teacup onto the edge of the coffee table, nestled her frame deeply into the cushions, and stared off across the room before offering an explanation. It was obvious that she was working herself up to something big.

"When you came to my door and I recognized who you were, I knew you were here about Byron. Maybe, in my heart, I knew you might come here someday. I suppose you could say that I expected you. I understand the pain you've suffered, Mr. Calley. Believe me, I understand it very well. Now, maybe we can help each other. Maybe I can answer some of your questions and you can help me answer some of mine. I'm afraid, Mr. Calley. I'm afraid of my son. I'm afraid of what he has become. I'm afraid of what he could do."

Her hands began to tremble; her eyes became large and damp. Without thinking, Bill reached over and laid his hand on the back of hers. She turned her hand over and grasped his tightly, then began to shake her head up and down.

"I'm so sorry about your daughter," she whispered.

"Thank you," he replied.

He waited a few moments before asking his next question — he wanted to be sure that she was ready. Calley had moved beyond his own curiosity, even beyond his passion for justice or retribution. All that mattered to him at this moment was the truth. He spoke with a slow, reassuring tone that he had always reserved for those closest to him.

"Can you tell me about your son, ma'am? I need to know if I've been chasing after the wrong man — if I've been wrong about all this. Is whatever's in that box going to tell me, one way or the other?"

"No, Mr. Calley. What's in that box will show you why I'm afraid of Byron and why others should be also. It won't give you the proof that you need. I don't have that. In my heart, I don't want to believe that Byron had anything to do with your daughter's death, but I don't know."

"Then, the box..." he said.

"It holds two scrapbooks and dozens of photographs, Mr. Calley. One of the scrapbooks has every clipping Byron could find about your daughter and the other girls who were murdered. Everything about the investigation. The other one is about the

Zodiac killer in the City. Everything he could find on the case. The photos are unpleasant, Mr. Calley... very unpleasant."

She turned away to face the far wall of the living room.

"There are photos in there... of my son and young girls, Mr. Calley..." she confessed in a barely audible voice. "Girls about the age of Elaine..."

Her chest began to shudder and the tears came without restraint. She pulled even further from him and slid to the end of the couch, squeezing herself against its arm and facing the wall with closed eyes. She was crying harder than she had since she was just a girl — a girl of about thirteen who had lost her very best friend.

Silent Partners

It was just after nine o'clock that night when Bill Calley returned home with the cardboard box that Jacqueline Avion had given him. His first order of business was to telephone Mick Millian and fill him in. Millian had been worried — very worried; he had expected to hear from Bill hours earlier and had called Calley's house several times. No one in the household knew when Bill would be back. No one was sure where he had gone.

When Bill finally called him, Millian was not in a listening mood. He demanded to know what had happened, if everything had gone as planned, and what Bill had learned. In all, Calley had spent nearly ten hours with Jacqueline and he had a hell of story to tell — far too much for a phone conversation. They needed to meet, and it couldn't be at the SCCID office. Millian told Bill he would be right over.

Calley had never looked at the contents of the box; after those first few moments of intense curiosity, he had never worked up the courage. After talking for hours with Jacqueline, he had simply replaced the flaps, retied the knot, and packed the box into the front seat of his car. When he got home, he slid it under the desk in his first-floor office. Jacqueline had told him all that he wanted to know about her son, or at least all that she *could* tell him. In fact, she had told him much more than he cared to know. Now, Bill didn't want to look at the photographs that Mrs. Avion claimed were inside the box. He didn't even want to think about them. That was a job for his friend at the SCCID.

In less than fifteen minutes, Calley was ushering Millian into the tiny downstairs bedroom that he had converted into an office after Elaine's murder. Mick was beside himself, hopping from one foot to the other, firing questions left and right without bothering to wait for an answer. Calley got his friend to settle down in a corner seat and commanded him to drink a large whiskey. Millian shot the drink back in a gulp and finally took a breath. Bill reached under the table in the center of the room and slid the cardboard box across the rug to a position midway between their feet. Millian's face went pale.

"Jesus, Bill!" He jumped to his feet. "Is that what I think it is?"

"Yeah, that belongs... belonged... to Avion," Bill nodded. "I guess it belongs to me now." Calley's expression was tight and worried.

"Holy shit! How did you get that?"

"Mrs. Avion gave it to me, Mick. I haven't looked inside, though."

Millian stared intently at the box, and then gave it a nudge with the toe of his left shoe. He bent over and examined the top of the box, its bindings, and the knot of white nylon rope. Then he sat back down, trying to resist the temptation to tear it apart and look inside.

"So, you don't know what's in there, right?"

"I didn't say that, Mick. I just said that I haven't looked inside the box. She told me what's in there. She told me a lot of stuff, Mick. I know there are photographs in there. Unpleasant ones, Mrs. Avion told me. Shots of her son with young girls. There are also newspaper clippings."

Millian looked up from the box and squinted.

"All right, Bill, what the hell is going on here? Jesus!" Mick was teetering just short of a full-blown explosion.

Calley turned and reached for the shelf behind him. He snagged the half-empty bottle of Jack Daniels just above his head and filled both their glasses. Then, he told his story. He talked for an hour — nonstop.

Jacqueline had told him things about her son that he had never expected to hear about anyone. She told him why Byron had never been able to form a close relationship with anyone but her, how he was always an outsider, even in his own home, always at the mercy of some one or another, always at odds and angry with the world. She talked about Byron's intense fear of his father, then, later, all men; his enduring hatred for women and his disdain for couples — especially young, intimate couples. Tearfully, she explained about Uncle Bob; her absentee husband, Frank; the lonely years at the Presidio in the City, Byron's high school debacles, his Navy failures, his miserable life, and her own profound guilt and terror. She told him why her son was never able to stay in one place for very long; how he would struggle with his sick sexual appetite and how it would inevitably overcome him, drive him to the other side of sane behavior, and force him to flee where he was living, usually returning home to her. She talked about his obsession with the Zodiac case, the Highway 101 Murders, and how he complained endlessly and bitterly about being a suspect in both investigations.

At the end of the day, after dark, after they had eaten ham and cheese sandwiches, Jacqueline told him about her son's most secret fears — those horrific living nightmares that broke through Byron's otherwise intractable exterior and made him as vulnerable as a child. She talked about black hoods and white nylon rope, like Uncle Bob used to have; she talked about hamsters, squirrels, secret symbols, and dark, windowless downstairs rooms — all the things that would go bump in the night and drive her son crazy with fear. She confessed to Bill how she had used those things against him, how she had kept him at a safe distance by returning again and again to the darkest corners of his psyche. Then she cried and asked for some kind of forgiveness, for some way of releasing herself from all that she had done — and all that she had failed to do.

In the end, Jacqueline shared Byron's most personal secrets and fears as openly as she was able, hour after hour, until she could go on no longer. However, what she was never able to share with Bill Calley was what she didn't know — an answer to the question that had brought him to her doorstep. Jacqueline had no idea where Byron was living, and when, if ever, he would be back. She didn't want to know. She didn't want him back in her home. However, she also admitted that Byron telephoned her regularly, usually on Sundays, usually in the afternoon. Would that help?

Millian was ready to rocket out of his chair a dozen times during Bill's saga, despite a second and third set of double Jacks to calm his nerves. The detective was exploding with questions but didn't want to interrupt. Bill was as intense and focused as Millian had ever seen him, and obviously on the far shores of exhaustion. It was clear that he couldn't be pushed, at all. The story had to come on its own.

When it was done, when Calley had slumped back into his chair and closed his eyes, Mick was ready to take over the conversation.

"God, Bill... I don't know where to begin. Listen, did you believe her? Did you buy it all? Was she telling you the truth?"

Calley slowly nodded with a sigh; yes, he believed her.

"All right," Mick said. "Okay... I think we need to look in that box. We need to see what's in there, Bill. Are you feeling up to that?"

Calley shook his head, his eyes still closed.

"Okay... How about if I look it over, Bill. Okay? How about if I go through the contents?"

"Yeah, that's what I want, Mick. I want *you* to do it. I sure the hell don't want to."

Mick slid from his chair and sat cross-legged in front of the box. He untied the knot at the top, carefully removed the strands and laid them aside, and pushed the flaps back to expose its contents. Then, he began to remove the items, one at a time, and place them on the floor. In the chair a few feet away, Bill Calley never moved, never opened his eyes. There was nothing going on in that room that he wanted to see. He had already vanished into that last, special Christmas — Elaine's Christmas.

The first item that Mick pulled from Avion's cardboard box was a red scrapbook with thick, black pages. It was the kind of scrapbook that had been designed for photographs, but Avion had put it to a different use. Across the cover of the book, in a rectangular area embellished with a pattern of intertwined gold flowers, someone had inscribed a huge letter "Z" with a black, felt-tip pen. Inside, the book contained page after page of articles meticulously clipped from the San Francisco *Chronicle*, the San Francisco *Examiner*, the Los Angeles *Times*, and the Vallejo *Times Herald*. All of them dealt with the Zodiac murders and the long, intense investigation that followed. The articles were arranged in chronological order, beginning with the oldest in 1969. In all, Mick counted more than sixty pages. Each of the pages held a single clipping, although a few of the longer articles spanned two pages. Each clipping had been carefully affixed to its page with scotch tape at the top so that it could be easily lifted to read the opposing side. There were no notes or other handwriting on any of the pages or on any of the clippings, except for two or three on which the date of the publication had been carefully printed by hand in the margin of the article. The last article in the scrapbook was seven months old.

Next out of the box was another scrapbook. This one had been wrapped in a piece of black cloth sewn into the crude shape of a sack. Folded, the cloth measured about two feet long and a foot or so wide. Tucked within the wrapping was the scrapbook. Like the Zodiac scrapbook, this one had a red cover, but no inscriptions or writing anywhere on its surface. Inside, the book contained a chronological account of the Highway 101 Murders and the investigation that followed each crime. All of the articles had appeared in the *Journal* and all had been put into the scrapbook in chronological order. The most recent was seven months old. Unlike the Zodiac clippings, which generally contained no markings, these articles held words and phrases that had been repeatedly emphasized by ruler-straight, blue-colored underlining here and there. More often than not, the words that were underlined were two names: Manny Bruin and Mick Millian.

Beneath the two scrapbooks, Mick found the last item in the box. It was an eleven-by-fourteen-inch manila envelope containing two-dozen photographs. The envelope was unmarked and unsealed. It was clear that it had been opened and closed many times. Mick slid the photographs from inside the envelope and pushed himself to his feet. He spread the images out on the table in Bill's office to examine them as closely as he could, being sure to handle them only by the edges. Most of the photographs were four-by-five inches in size, although three of them were eight-by-tens. All of them were in color. All were amateurish.

What Mick saw in those images sent him into an immediate, red-faced rage. Before him was a series of shots of Byron Avion with four different girls. In most of the photographs, the parties were nude and in some form of physical contact, although there was nothing to indicate intercourse. Three of the shots showed Avion naked, while the girl who stood or knelt beside him was clad only in panties. It was obvious that all the photos had been taken in the same location, in and around a double-size, blue-sheeted bed pushed up against a plain white or off-white wall. There was no other furniture in the photograph and no way of determining the location or time. The impression given by the images was that the shot had been taken by a 35-mm camera posted on a tripod with a timer mechanism.

Millian stared again at each of the images. The four girls in the photographs looked young — very young. The Detective's guess was that none of them was over sixteen; one of them could **have been much younger, perhaps only twelve or thirteen. In one** of the photographs taken with the youngest girl, Avion held a black object in his left hand. It looked very much like the black cloth sack that was wrapped around the second scrapbook.

Mick reached down to the floor and grabbed the black cloth. He held it up to eye level, and then reached inside to spread it apart with his hands. As he turned it around to get a good look at all sides, he realized that two diamond-shaped holes had been neatly cut into the fabric. It looked like a hood of some type. Quickly, he pulled one of the photographs from the table and held it close. Yes, it looked like the same kind of hood as in the photo. It was a goddamn sex toy of some kind, and Avion had kept it as a remembrance!

"Sick shit..." Millian grumbled as he shook his head. He was standing in the center of the room with the black hood in one hand and the photo in the other, wearing a furious scowl.

"Do I want to know what you're looking at, Mick? It doesn't sound very good. I don't think I want to know..." Bill whispered from his chair, eyes still closed.

"Elaine's not in any of these photos, Bill. They're older photos, I think. No one in here that we know, okay? Nothing here that can hurt you." His voice was soothing and controlled.

"Yeah... well... that's good, but it doesn't make it okay, does it? Somebody's in those pictures... somebody's been hurt..."

"No, Bill, it doesn't make it okay. You're right. Somebody's in these pictures. Somebody's been hurt. Nothing's going to be okay as long as this sick fuck is on the street!" Bill knew all too well where this would lead and he wasn't ready to deal with it. He needed to be away from his old friend, away from everyone for a while.

"Mick, I can't handle any more of this tonight. I'm exhausted. I need to get some sleep." Calley pulled himself out of his chair with a grunt, briefly laid his hand on Mick's shoulder, and headed for the door. He paused at the threshold and turned slightly.

"Stay here tonight, Mick. I know you've got some work to do. Why not stay here? I'll see you in the morning and we can talk. It would be good to have you here in the morning."

Calley didn't wait for an answer. He turned and headed upstairs, to the spare bedroom. Without undressing, he laid across the unused bed and fell into a numb, painless, thankful sleep.

The next morning came much too fast. With it arrived all the pain of the previous day, all the new worries, all of the confusion. Bill struggled down the stairs, still dressed in yesterday's clothes, and stepped into the office to find Millian slumped in his chair, snoring. On his lap were the photographs.

"Hey, Mick, want some coffee?" Bill asked.

"Huh?" Millian mumbled, rubbing his eyes. "What?"

"Want some coffee?"

Mick shook his head slightly, and opened his eyes as wide as he was able. From the detective's groggy perspective, Bill looked even worse than the night before.

"Jesus! You look like shit, Bill."

"Okay... okay... so do you. You want some coffee or not?" Calley answered in mock anger.

Millian nodded and smiled but said nothing. Instead, he grabbed the photographs, moved to the table, and spread them out, just as he had done a dozen times during the night. Calley left the room to make some fresh coffee. When he returned, Millian was still hovering over the images.

"Here," Calley said, setting the mug on the edge of the table. He slumped down into the chair that Mick had occupied the night before and stared at his friend. Millian grabbed the mug and moved away from the table. He settled into the opposing chair and began to sip, his eyes still heavy and dark from lack of sleep.

"What's going on here, Mick?" Bill asked in a slow monotone. "What's the deal with Avion? You know, I thought I had a pretty good idea about him before I talked to his mother. Now, I don't know what to think. I have no idea what or who this guy is."

"Well, you can think this," Mick shot back. "The guy is fucked up, isn't he? I mean, he has a real problem with young girls. That's obvious. I'm sure it runs a hell of a lot deeper."

Calley shook his head in disgust. "Mick, I don't want to get into the anger part of this thing right now. There's been too much of that already. I just want to know what the fuck is going on... *please*, just help me understand this..."

Millian couldn't remember the last time he heard his friend use the word "fuck" or plead for help. For one of the few times in his life, he was speechless. Finally, after several seconds, he made an attempt.

"Listen, I'm sorry, Bill. I'm sorry about my whole attitude. I'm sorry about sending you over there. Jesus! Let's start all over again, all right?"

Calley nodded his approval and gave his friend a half-smile.

"Okay, Bill. What we have here is a guy who's into some kinky sex with young girls. That's clear enough; but, I admit, that doesn't make him a killer. It doesn't mean he had anything to do with Elaine. But... it does mean that we have a good reason to go after him and find out what's going on in his life. We have enough for that. And I think... if we're careful..."

Calley pushed himself to the edge of the chair and gave the detective a troubled, quizzical stare. "What do you mean, you *think*... if we're *careful*..." he echoed. "What does *that* mean, Mick?"

"It means two things, Bill. First, these photos may or may not constitute some kind of evidence of a violation. On the face of it, they seem strong. But, you've got to remember how we came onto these photos. It wasn't exactly kosher, was it? I mean, what we have here may or may not interest the district attorney, get it?"

Bill nodded in an unsteady, frustrated way. He understood what Mick was saying, but he didn't like it.

"Listen, Bill, it's not *all* bad news," Millian added. "There's enough here to pick Avion up and question him. That's for sure. Whether or not we can do more... well... we have to work that out later. There's another problem, too. Maybe a worse one..."

"Yeah, I know," Calley interrupted. "How do you get this stuff to your boss without getting your goose cooked, right?"

Millian nodded and offered his friend a smile. "Yeah, you said it. Now that we have something interesting, getting it to Manny in the right way is what we need to work out. I don't suppose Avion's mother would be of any help there, would she? I mean, would she be willing to produce this stuff... give it over to the SCCID on her own?"

"I didn't ask her, Mick, but I don't think so. In fact, I'm certain. She didn't want anyone else to even see what's in the box, although she did say that I could do whatever I thought was right with it. She knows about you. She knows we're friends, so maybe you're an exception in her mind, maybe not. I don't know. I know this: I don't want to put her in jeopardy, Mick. I don't want to be responsible for that."

Millian nodded. "Yeah, all right... I can see why she wouldn't want to be involved, being afraid of him and all that kind of thing.

Makes sense to me... We need to come up with something that works... something better."

Bill leaned back in his chair, closed his eyes, and rubbed his hand across his mouth and chin. Across the room, Millian stared at him, sensing that he was struggling with some kind of decision.

"Mick, I'm going to bring all this stuff to Manny myself."

"Wait a min..." Millian jumped from his chair.

Calley silenced him with a wave of his hand.

"That's what I *want* to do, Mick, and I really don't want to argue about it. This is my stuff. I've worked hard to get it. I'm tired of the games. I'm going to take it to Manny. I'll keep your name out of it — you know I will. But my mind's made up and that's that."

Millian nodded reluctantly and dropped his head. There was no point pressing him any further. Bill's mind was made up.

Late Summer, 1974
The Arrangements

Calley was shocked at how well Manny reacted to his involvement with the Avion matter. He had expected a tongue-lashing, at least, but it never came. The pair spent hours in the SCCID conference room, going over each detail of his encounter with Jacqueline Avion, how he came into possession of Byron's effects, and all that he had learned about the suspect's background.

Naturally, Bruin was most interested in the contents of the box, particularly the photographs and the second scrapbook in which his name and that of his partner played such a prominent role. Throughout their conversation, Bruin was typically reserved, polite, and careful, but Bill also discovered that he was a sincere, sensitive man who had taken a much deeper and personal interest in Elaine's death than he had ever imagined. By the end of the day, Calley felt an unspoken friendship with Bruin that he had never expected. It was a discovery that Bill would come to treasure over the years ahead.

Calley's greatest concern — that he would be forced to reveal Mick's involvement — never materialized. Manny had asked about Mick's role in Calley's meeting with Jacqueline, along with how Bill had acquired such a detailed knowledge of Byron's existence. Bill answered these questions with as few words as possible, and those that he uttered were painfully vague. What surprised Calley was that Bruin never pressed the point. He just accepted a series of obviously diffuse answers and moved on. Although Bill was curious about this, he was also very grateful. Perhaps Manny's crooked half-smile — the one that always seemed to follow each of Bill's vague responses — said it all.

For Bruin, the bottom line of his meeting with Bill Calley was not *how* he had come into possession of the scrapbooks and photographs, or even why, but what the SCCID was going to do about them now that they had surfaced. It was a tricky question, riddled with legal and political pitfalls. Manny was faced with two problems that needed to be addressed right away: how to locate Byron Avion and, assuming that he *could* find him, how to prosecute him for a crime based on the contents of the box.

Bill Calley had a solution to the first problem. Jacqueline told Bill that her son often called her on Sunday afternoons. That was the opening Bruin needed. Now, the detective wanted to know if Bill would be willing to ask Mrs. Avion to have her son come for a visit. According to Manny's plan, Jacqueline would ask Byron the next time he called to come by her home. She could use the excuse that she would be traveling again soon and would like to see him before she left.

At first, Calley was cool to the idea. He had never intended to go back to the Avion house or to speak with Jacqueline under these kinds of circumstances. Beyond that, given Jacqueline's fear of her son, he wasn't sure that she would go along with the plan anyway. But Manny was persuasive and determined, and it did seem like the best way to solve the problem. Bill agreed to give it a try.

On the first Saturday morning in August 1974, Calley called on Mrs. Avion to present her with the idea. He was more than mildly surprised when she quickly agreed, under one condition. Jacqueline didn't want to be in the house, or even in the area, when her son came calling. The SCCID would have to arrest her son outside her home, before he entered, and without any reference to her involvement. It would have to be that way, or Jacqueline would forget the whole thing.

Calley phoned Bruin that afternoon, as soon as he returned home from visiting Mrs. Avion, and told him the news. Like Jacqueline, Manny agreed to the conditions with no argument, and Calley finalized the deal with a second call to Mrs. Avion. She would call Bill as soon as she heard from her son and had worked out a time for him to visit. However, she would not talk to anyone else, especially anyone from the SCCID, about her involvement. Everything had to go through Bill.

That night, in the darkness of his tiny office, Calley poured himself several more drinks than he needed. He spent hours wondering how he had managed to make himself a spokesman for the mother of the man who may have killed his daughter.

Three weeks passed without any word from Jacqueline Avion. Bruin and Millian kept in constant contact with Calley, asking what he had heard, wondering what was going on, and "just checking in." Bill's report was always the same — nothing. Occasionally, Manny would urge Calley to call Mrs. Avion, just to be sure that she was still on track and willing to play along with their plan. Calley persistently refused, saying that he would only call her after a month had passed. He assured Bruin that Jacqueline would be true to her word, although secretly he wasn't sure.

During those long, frustrating weeks, Mick continued to hover around, although he made sure to keep as much of the pressure off as he was able. Millian could sense the tension in Bill and he wasn't about to make the situation worse than it already was. Patience was never Mick's strong point, but he showed enormous amounts of it throughout the rest of August.

In the early evening of the last Sunday in August, Bill received a phone call from Mrs. Avion. She had spoken to her son a few hours earlier but had needed some time to think about whether or not she really wanted to go through with the agreement. In the end, Jacqueline's word proved to be as good as Calley had hoped. The news she gave him was even better. Byron had agreed to come and visit her. He would arrive about ten in the morning on the following Sunday — the first Sunday in September. Jacqueline told Bill that she would be away from her home that day. So, whatever he had planned with Millian and Bruin would have to happen without her.

Bill thanked her, reassured her that she was doing the right thing, and hung up with a penetrating ache in his stomach. His next call was to Mick. Like Jacqueline before him, Bill put the ball squarely in Millian's court, which was just what the detective had hoped for.

An hour later, Millian and Bruin were together at Manny's house, making plans. As usual, Mick couldn't sit still through Bruin's hours of assessing and reassessing. In the end, they agreed on the basics, but not without a good deal of heated bantering. Come the following Sunday, the detectives would pluck Avion off the street and place him in custody. They would do it in front of Jacqueline's home, and they would do it as quietly as possible.

Then, once they had him in hand, they would try to figure out what to do with him.

Chameleon in a Sport Jacket

Millian and Bruin sat in an uneasy silence, in the front seat of the year-old beige van that Mick had checked out of the SCCID car pool. The pair had hardly exchanged a word since they arrived at the stakeout. Both were lost in private visions of what might lie ahead and how each would handle Avion when they finally encountered him. Both knew that the man they had hunted for so many months was unpredictable and potentially violent. As usual, Bruin had been endlessly preoccupied with the details — the little things that could make or break their stakeout. He had even decided that their usual ride, the blue sedan, would be too obvious for the occasion and far too familiar to Avion. It was Mick who had suggested the van, something more in keeping with the times and the neighborhood.

Earlier that morning, the detectives had parked their well-scrubbed vehicle across the street from Jacqueline's house, midway up the block. It sat inconspicuously under the umbrella of a thick, leafy oak that had overgrown a good portion of the street and cracked and distorted the narrow sidewalk. Through the front window of the shaded vehicle, it was easy for Bruin to keep an eye on Jacqueline Avion's porch and the street beyond her house.

Millian watched the other direction from the van's two rear windows.

Just after ten that morning, Millian saw Avion approaching. At first, the detective wasn't sure that it was really him. They had expected their man to arrive in some kind of a vehicle. The individual strolling up the street toward Jacqueline's house had appeared from around the far corner on foot. Then, there was the outfit. The last time Millian had seen Avion, he was donned in his customary dark windbreaker, military-style pants, and boots. The man moving toward them was dressed in a nicely tailored, gray sport jacket, black slacks, and a white shirt unbuttoned at the collar.

"Jesus, Manny, look at this!" Millian squawked. "Is that him? Can that be him? Man... he sure looks different."

Bruin swung quickly around and peered out the window, squinting into the morning sunlight. "Yeah, I think so..." he mumbled. "Sure doesn't look like the last time we saw him, eh? I think it's him..."

Millian continued to watch him. His pace was even and easy, not determined and quick as he remembered Avion's. There was nothing hurried in his demeanor, nothing tense, rushed, or untoward. He looked like a man who was taking a leisurely stroll after a Sunday church service. Millian scanned him for signs of a weapon, but his hands were empty, swinging gently in front of him as he moved along the sidewalk. As he strode closer, within a few yards of the van, Millian got a good look at his face.

"Okay, Manny, that's definitely him. That's Avion. You ready?" he asked excitedly, keeping his eyes fixed on Avion, lest his prey should somehow vanish.

Bruin nodded and swung around in his seat. They opened their doors at the same time, stepped out of the vehicle, and walked briskly across the street in Avion's direction, approaching him at a 45-degree angle. As they reached the sidewalk and stood within a few feet of their target, the man in the sport jacket slowed his pace and looked thoughtfully at Millian, ignoring his partner.

"Hello, Detective," he said with a friendly smile. "It's been a while, hasn't it? I *do* know you. I can't recall just when..."

"Mr. Avion, we need to talk to you," Bruin announced. By now, both detectives were directly in front of the suspect, blocking his way. The man in the sport jacket stood motionless but relaxed, his hands by his sides.

"Yes, well, that's fine. You can talk to me if you like. You're Detective Bruin, correct?" he asked, turning his head to the shorter man. Avion wore a strange, distant expression. His smile was still warm and genuine, not at all like his trademark smirk.

"That's right, I'm Manny Bruin, Mr. Avion. I'm sure you remember the last..."

"Not clearly, I'm afraid." He rubbed the side of his face with a burly right hand, furrowing his brow and studying them. After a moment, he began to slowly roll his head from left to right and back again. "No, I'm sorry, I can't remember specifically."

Millian was clearly running out of patience with this unexpected and, to his way of thinking, unnecessary dialogue. He was obviously confused at Avion's reaction and not ready to accept what he had just heard. Mick hopped nervously from foot to foot and blurted out what he had waited to announce for a long, long time.

"Byron Avion, we're arresting you..."

"What!?" Avion yelped, cutting him off. "I'm not Byron Avion and I haven't done anything! Why would you want to arrest *me*?"

Millian took a step backward. He stared at the man, then at Bruin. The younger detective's expression was pained and disoriented. It was time for his partner to take over.

"Mr. Avion, there seems to be some confusion here," Bruin said, in a soothing tone. "You *are* Byron Avion, correct?"

The man in the sport jacket shook his head with enough energy to jiggle his plentiful jowls. "No. My name is *Frank* Avion, Detective. I'm not *Byron* Avion."

"Oh bullshit!" Millian spouted. He jumped a step closer and bent at the hips in a gesture of defiance. "What kind of game is this?"

Avion looked stunned and hurt, but not combative. His eyes grew smaller and darted back and forth between the detectives. He wore a fearful, timid expression that neither Bruin nor Millian had seen before, and certainly hadn't expected to see from Byron Avion. Manny squeezed Mick's arm. It was a clear signal: shut up!

"All right, Frank," Bruin resumed, in a practiced monotone. "May I call you Frank?"

Avion nodded. His upper lip had become damp and Manny could see a trembling along the outlines of his face. He was truly afraid. This was no act.

"We need to find Byron Avion," Bruin continued, searching for a way to put the big man at ease. "We need to talk to him. Can you help us do that, Frank?"

"No," he answered in a terse, anxious voice. "I don't know about him, Detective. I can't tell you about him."

"All right, then... tell me why *you* are here today, Frank? Why did you come here?"

"I'm coming to visit my mother, Detective. She's going away on a trip and wanted me to visit her today. I sometimes visit her, you know. I call her regularly. We keep in touch..." His voice trailed off to a whisper as he looked beyond Millian's shoulder in the direction of Jacqueline's house.

"Okay, Frank. You're here to visit Jacqueline, right? And she's your mother, right?"

He nodded at Bruin uncertainly, trying unsuccessfully to regain his earlier smile.

"Is Byron coming here today, too? Will he be visiting your mother today?" Bruin asked, as gently as he could.

Avion looked directly at the detective in a pained, pleading way. "I suppose so," he said. "I guess so. You need to ask my mother about that to be sure."

Once more, Millian started hopping from foot to foot, out of patience and ready to take matters into his own hands. Bruin wasn't about to give him the chance.

"Mr. Avion, perhaps we've made a mistake here. If so, I certainly apologize. Could you give us a moment? Let me talk to my partner for a moment, if you don't mind. Please just wait here, okay? I think we can clear this all up."

"Yes," Avion said, dropping his head to stare at the sidewalk. He looked like a child who had been caught with his hand in the cookie jar. It was clear that he wasn't going anywhere without permission.

Bruin pulled Mick brusquely by the arm and walked him up the block toward Jacqueline's front door. When they were out of earshot, he turned to face Avion, now several yards away, and covered his mouth with the back of his right hand.

"Listen, Mick..." Bruin began.

"All right, Manny, what the fuck is going on here?" Millian demanded in a loud whisper. "You know this guy is just jerking us around, don't you? Jesus! Let's just haul his ass in and be done with it!"

Manny nodded and turned to face his partner. "Probably, Mick, but that doesn't matter right now. You and I know that this guy is Byron Avion. Maybe he knows it too and he's just playing a game on us. It doesn't matter, Mick. We don't have much here, do we? We had better use finesse, my friend, not a bulldozer, if we want to make this work. Understand me?"

Bruin's face was set in stone. This was not the time to argue. Mick nodded, a look of disgust crossing his face.

"Okay, Mick. Let's get back to him. *Please*, just let me do this my way. You play along but keep your famous temper in your back pocket, will you?" The words were harsh but there was the shadow of a smile across Manny's lips. They walked briskly back to Avion.

"Why do you want to arrest me, Detective?" the big man asked Millian. "Why do you want to do that?"

Mick looked quickly at Manny, then back at Avion. It was time for a change in tactics. "I'm sorry about that, Frank. Maybe I have you confused with... er... Byron. Is he your brother, Frank?"

Avion shook his head slowly. "I don't know..." He looked away, in the direction of Jacqueline's house. The expression on his face was the picture of simplicity, like that of a child just after waking.

Millian tried to steer a different course, to bring him back to the conversation.

"Frank, where's your car? Where did you park it?" the detective asked, moving a little closer.

"I don't drive, Detective. I don't have a car."

"Well... how did you get here then?" Millian prodded, struggling not to sound angry.

"I walked here. I got a ride. I walked some more... I don't know..."

"Okay, Frank... Did Byron come with you today? Is he coming along too?"

"I don't know about Byron... that much." The big man looked back with a fearful, uncertain stare. "I hope you aren't going to arrest me for something *he* did? You're not going to arrest me, are you?"

Millian wagged his head no.

"No, Frank, we won't do anything like that," Bruin piped in. "But... we would like you to help us with our investigation. Would you be willing to do that?"

Avion's expression changed from anxiety to glee. He smiled elegantly at the detectives and seemed to stand a bit taller.

"Oh, sure, I'd be happy to do that!" he said. "Yes, indeed. Help you with an investigation?"

"Yes, help us with an investigation," Manny confirmed. "It's an important investigation, Frank, and we could sure use the help. Are you are willing to do this?"

"Yes sir, I am," Avion answered. "You bet I am!"

Millian stared at the man. If this guy was acting, he was the best that Millian had ever met. But if he was the suspect, Mick wanted to reach out and grab him by the balls — give him something he'd always remember. Mick shuffled his head from side to side, signaling his disbelief and frustration. Avion caught that gesture and reacted instantly.

"Detective Millian?" he asked, looking squarely at Mick.

"Yes..."

"You don't seem to like me very much, do you?"

Millian stayed silent, a flush of red racing across his cheeks. From Manny's perspective, his partner's control at that moment was nothing short of remarkable.

"I don't think it's very fair to dislike someone you don't even know, do you?" Avion scolded. "That's not very nice..."

Mick's eyes grew wide and as confused as those of the man standing in front of him. All he could do was stare back.

That Day
SCCID Interrogation Room

When Bruin, Millian, and Avion arrived at the SCCID office twenty minutes later, Manny escorted his suspect into the first-floor interrogation room. It was a generous affair, with a broad, thick window that looked out on the hallway between Bruin's office and an open area for the desks of field officers. Today, the office was desolate, manned only by an aging, overweight sergeant at the front desk and a couple officers who had nothing left in the way of a home life.

During the ride there, Avion had not spoken a word. He peered out the passenger's window, occasionally bobbing his head and making light, whistling sounds. He seemed alarmingly disinterested in what was going on around him. Once he reached the office, however, he became animated and chatty, asking questions and carefully examining his surroundings.

After getting Avion settled in the interrogation room, Bruin offered him fresh coffee and two-day-old doughnuts from the SCCID supply, along with the opportunity to telephone his mother and a promise that he would soon fetch the case material on the aforementioned investigation. Avion seemed content, but a bit perturbed that he hadn't been able to get through to Jacqueline. He couldn't understand why no one was answering the phone when she had invited him over to spend the day. However, by the time Manny left the interrogation room to gather up the case files, Avion had given up on the idea. He munched happily on a stale doughnut and sipped an anemic mixture of coffee and milk. Outside the room, Millian was anxiously waiting for his partner.

"Hey, Mick, I need something here," Bruin said, trying to intercept the expected barrage of questions. "I want you to call Cindy Turgell and that shrink, Freeman or Friedman, or whatever his name is. I want you to get them both down here right away to help us out with this guy." Bruin nodded toward the interrogation room. Millian could see Avion sitting at the gray metal table, oblivious to their conversation.

"Yeah, I'll do that, Manny. Right away. But first you've got to tell me if you think this shit is real or what? Is this guy really that whacked out?"

Manny shrugged his shoulders. "Honestly, Mick, I have no idea. If he's faking, he's doing a great job. If it's real, I don't know what the hell is wrong with him and I have no idea what to do with him. That's why I want Turgell and the shrink to get down here. They've got to help us figure out what we've got here." Manny's expression was drawn and worried.

"Okay, done," said Mick. He turned from his partner and headed down the hallway. When he arrived at Bruin's office, the detective closed the door and dialed Cynthia Turgell at home. He briefly explained the problem and asked her to get down there ASAP and, oh yeah, please bring that shrink, Freeman or Friedman, or whatever his name was. She agreed, with a hint of grumbling, reminding him that it *was* Sunday. She said she would bring the shrink, and that his name was *Fryman* — Samuel Fryman.

Millian thanked her, hung up, and returned to Bruin outside the interrogation room. He informed Manny that Turgell would be arriving with the shrink as quickly as she could. In the meantime, they agreed that they had to keep Avion occupied. The last thing they wanted was for their suspect to become uncomfortable or suspicious, or decide that he needed an attorney, which would immediately force an end to the interview. The pair decided that Manny should take the first round while Millian waited outside the room with the door open, just in case the suspect's mood took a change for the worse. They agreed that there was no point in agitating their guest, and Avion seemed more comfortable with Bruin than his partner.

Manny entered the interrogation room and pulled his chair up to the table, directly across from Avion. The big man was just finishing the last of his coffee. He looked up at the detective and smiled.

"You want some more of that?" Bruin offered.

"No, thanks, Detective. Not right now. Maybe later. Did you bring the files with you? Do you want to talk to me about the investigation now?" Avion was shuffling around in his chair with anticipation.

"The files are on the way, Frank," Bruin answered. "They'll be here soon. In the meantime, maybe you can tell me what you know about these crimes here, in Santa Rosa... about the kidnapping and the murders. Can you fill me in on the details? Maybe there's something we've overlooked."

Avion nodded and smiled knowingly. "Sure, I've kept up on everything. I've been following it closely. I've also been following the San Francisco investigation. I have scrapbooks with everything, Detective. The problem is that I've misplaced them. I can't remember where they've gone." He dropped his head and stared at the table, fiddled with the empty Styrofoam cup until he snapped a large triangular piece from its lip. Finally, he looked up sheepishly and stared at Bruin. "I wish I could remember where I left them... I'm sorry."

"Well, that's all right. Maybe I can help you, Frank. Let me get something to show you. Okay? It's something that I think you'll want to see."

The big man nodded his agreement but never changed his expression. He seemed ashamed or embarrassed.

Manny stepped out of the room and headed for his office. There, he removed the two scrapbooks from the cardboard box that Jacqueline Avion had given to Bill Calley. He left the manila envelope with the photographs and the black cloth hood on his desk. When Bruin rejoined Avion, he placed the scrapbooks at the edge of the table, just out of reach, facing his suspect. The big man immediately jumped out of his chair, leaned across the table, and pulled the two books toward him.

"Oh, yes!" he yelped. "Here they are!" He picked up the scrapbooks and held them to his chest, rubbing the palm of his hand across the outside of each. "Where did you find them?"

Bruin sat back in his chair and thought for a moment — a moment too long. Avion's smile turned to a dark frown.

"Where did you get them?" Avion demanded. "Where?!"

"From your mother," Bruin answered, staring back. The detective instantly regretted his answer, but it was too late. He waited for Avion to react, bracing himself for some kind of angry onslaught. For the first time during the interview, Bruin considered the fastest way out of the room.

Instead, Avion slumped back in his chair, cocked his head, and began to aimlessly scan the ceiling. For some time, his eyes roamed back and forth, as if he were trying to settle on some memory, some vision of when he had last been in possession of the scrapbooks. Then he smiled again, and calmly returned his gaze to the man across the table.

"Oh, all right. My mother had them. She had my books. She has all my things. That makes sense, Detective. I just don't recall when..."

Avion left his statement dangling, and began leafing through the first scrapbook, which contained dozens of Santa Rosa *Journal* articles about the Highway 101 Murders. He turned each page as if it were part of a sacred manuscript, pausing to study the words and ensuring that each piece had been well affixed to its background. After several moments, he closed the scrapbook and carefully placed it between himself and Bruin, its cover facing the detective.

"It's not complete, Detective, is it? I mean, it ends several months ago," he grumbled. "I wish I understood that..."

"Yes, Frank, that's right. It's not complete. Can you tell me why? Do you have any idea why?"

Avion shook his head, clearly upset.

"How about the other scrapbook, Frank? Is that one yours too?" Manny asked, pointing at the other book.

The big man glanced at the red book with the large "Z" inscribed across its face. He ran his hand gently across its surface and stared off somewhere beyond the interrogation room.

"Yes," he replied. "That's mine."

"Do you want to look it over, Frank?"

"No. No need to look it over. It's not my favorite. The other one is."

Manny stood up and began to pace as quietly as he could. He was waiting for some kind of lead, some idea of where to take the conversation. He could sense that the big man was growing impatient and uncomfortable with the silence. Finally, he decided that the best idea at hand was the scrapbooks. At least they held Avion's interest.

"Frank, these are both *your* scrapbooks, correct?"

"Correct," came the reply, accompanied by a generous head bob.

"Okay. Did Byron have anything to do with them? Did he help you with them?"

"Absolutely not!" he snapped, shaking his head. "These are *mine*, Detective!"

"Okay, I understand," Bruin assured him.

Manny sat down in his chair with a tight smile; he looked directly at Avion. "Yes, I see, Frank. These are *your* scrapbooks and you gave them to your mother to keep for you? You gave her your other things, too, right?"

Avion nodded uncertainly. He didn't agree. He didn't disagree. His mind was on something else, something more interesting.

"Detective, when can we go over the investigation?" he pleaded. "You said you needed my help and I'm ready to give that to you. When do we start?" Once again, his eyes were wide and bright with anticipation.

Bruin gulped noisily and raced for an answer — an excuse, or anything that wouldn't set him off again. The seconds began to stretch out uncomfortably. Fortunately, the detective never had to answer.

"Manny, I'm sorry to interrupt." Millian pushed by the half-open door. He offered Avion a curt smile but received only a blank stare in return.

"Yeah, Mick, what's up?" Bruin replied.

"The other members of the investigation team are here."

"Good, good!" Bruin exclaimed. "Frank, we're working with a few others on the investigation. We do this with all big cases. It gives us a broader perspective — less opportunity to miss something important. Would you like to meet the rest of the team and talk to them? I think you'd find it very interesting. Maybe you could be of some help here." Manny tried to sound as excited as possible.

"I would!" Avion chirped, his eyes searching the doorway. "That would be good. Very good!"

Bruin excused himself with a smile and stepped into the hallway, closing the door behind him. Outside the interrogation room, Millian was waiting with Cynthia Turgell and Sam Fryman.

"Cindy, thanks for coming down on such short notice." He put his hand on her shoulder. "I could sure use some help here."

"No problem, Manny. This is Sam Fryman." She nodded at the chubby, balding man next to her. "I'm sure you remember..."

"Yeah, sure, I remember," Bruin interrupted, offering his hand. "Thanks for helping us out here. We could sure use your expertise."

Fryman nodded and gave the detective a strong pump of his hand.

"So, Manny, what do you need?" Turgell asked. "What can we do?"

"I'd like Mick to fill Sam in on our guy in the box over there," he replied, tilting his head toward the interrogation room. "Mick has some material in my office to show Sam and he needs to provide some background on our suspect. The bottom line is this: I have no idea if this guy is jerking us around or if he has some kind of psychological problem. I don't want to leave him alone in there for too long, so Mick will give you the details while Cindy and I talk to him for a while."

"What I need, Sam, is to know what's going on with this man. He's a suspect in some probable crimes dealing with children, and maybe a lot more. But, I need to know as much as I can about his state of mind and what he knows about the crimes that Mick will tell you about. Okay? I need to keep him talking to me."

Fryman nodded but remained silent. Bruin noticed his eyes. They were unusually large, deep brown and constantly moving, scanning his surroundings. He was obviously a man of few words, but it was also clear that he missed nothing within his range. It struck the detective that this was a fellow who wouldn't need to hear anything twice. Bruin searched his memory for when they had worked together, what cases had joined them in the past, but he couldn't recall.

"What about me, Manny?" Cindy asked. "This is way out of my league. I don't know what I can do for you."

"No, it's not out of your league, Cindy. I need two things from you. First, I want your opinion on what this guy knows about the murders, especially some of the forensic details. On one hand, I think he may know more than he's saying; on the other, he claims to know *everything*. I need your opinion on what he really knows and what he's making up, or what he's just picked up from the media."

"And the other thing..." she prompted.

"I need to know if this guy is bullshitting me or not, Cindy. Mick thinks he might be, and I don't know. I want your gut level reaction. I know that Sam here will be the best judge of that, but I want *your* opinion, too. One way or the other, I need to know what's going on with this guy, what he knows and what he doesn't know. Most of all, I need to separate the bullshit from the facts, and that's where you shine in my book."

"Yeah, that's fine, Manny, if that's what you want," she answered, fighting back a blush. "I'll do what I can. You know that."

"Okay, good," Bruin said. "Sam, do you mind going with Mick into my office? You two can chat for a while and Mick can show you some of the evidence that may link this guy to the recent crimes. He can also give you the background you need to talk to him. I should need you in about a half-hour or so. You okay with that?"

"Sure, that's fine," Fryman replied, flatly.

Mick tapped Fryman on the arm and led him into Bruin's office, closing the door behind them.

"So, Cindy, are you ready to meet Suspect Zero?" Manny asked.

"Suspect Zero?"

"Yeah, well, I don't know what else to call him. He's telling me that he's not who I think he is, and, frankly, he's got me confused as hell. He's a suspect. He's a zero. Maybe you can help me figure out what else I've got in there..."

Turgell scrunched her face and twirled a finger through her red curls.

"Wow! What a way to spend a Sunday! You sure know how to show a girl a good time, Manny."

Bruin gave her a shrug and as much of a smile as he could manage.

Turgell and Bruin spent nearly an hour with Avion and learned little, at least in a traditional sense. It was clear that the big man was familiar with most of the details of the Highway 101 Murders, including times, dates, names, and places. However, there was nothing in what he said that led Turgell to believe that he had any special knowledge. Avion was chatty, open, and more than willing to answer questions, especially those posed by Cindy. He also threw out a few of his own, particularly to Turgell, which she had to sidestep in order to preserve the integrity of the case.

At one point, Avion referred to his beloved scrapbook and asked if Turgell cared to look it over. She politely agreed and spent several moments leafing through its pages. Looking at those articles convinced Turgell that Avion had one heck of a memory, perhaps even a photographic memory. Throughout their conversation, he was able to provide specific dates and facts that he had probably gleaned from the *Journal* articles.

Turgell came away from the meeting convinced that Avion was not the killer, although she had no explanation for why he denied his true identity. When Bruin asked Cindy if she thought he was lying or playing some kind of game, she was unsure but didn't think so. Was he whacked out in the head? She wasn't sure about that either. She could only say that she saw nothing in him that seemed unusually violent and heard nothing that led her to believe that he had anything to do with the crimes. To her, the guy seemed like more of voyeur than anything else. She could certainly understand why Manny referred to him as "Suspect Zero."

At the end of the interview, Bruin offered Avion some more coffee and doughnuts, and told him he was ready to fetch the other member of their team, if he wasn't too tired to continue. Avion made it clear that he was eager to continue, and started in on another donut.

Millian had had more than enough time to brief Sam Fryman on Avion. They had gone over his background and had briefly reviewed the Highway 101 Murders. Then, the pair examined the photographs and black cloth hood that was left behind in Bruin's office. Mick also described the scrapbooks that Avion kept, telling the psychologist that they were now in the interrogation room with the suspect.

The photographs proved to be especially important to Fryman. He spent a good deal of time examining each of them. The psychologist wanted to take them into the interrogation room with him and use them to elicit some kind of response. Millian agreed that this was a good idea. He also emphasized that his partner wanted to keep Avion talking, and to avoid alienating him or prompting him to terminate the interview by asking for legal representation. Fryman said he understood. The overall strategy of the meeting would be a simple one, like the one Bruin had used — get Avion's trust, get him talking, and find out what he knows. For Fryman, the other pursuit was to discover what game this guy was playing — or, if it wasn't a game, to find out what it was.

When Manny returned to his office to get Sam Fryman, the psychologist asked if he could meet with Avion alone. At first, Bruin was reluctant, concerned that his suspect was unpredictable and possibly dangerous. But Fryman insisted, making it clear that if he was to gain Avion's trust, he had to do it alone and in a confidential setting. Bruin agreed, so long as the door to the interrogation room remained open and he was outside, along with Millian. They promised to stay out of Avion's sight but within ready range should anything go wrong. Fryman felt that this was a good arrangement and agreed. He and Bruin went straight to the interrogation room where Manny introduced him as "the man who is helping us to understand the motives and behavior of the individual who murdered these girls." As Bruin left the room, it was clear that Fryman had Avion's complete attention, if not awe.

For more than an hour, Millian and Bruin hovered near the open door, just beyond sight, listening to the muffled voices inside. Manny had tried to send Cynthia Turgell home, but she had insisted on waiting until the interview was finished so she could talk to her colleague. The trio spent their time pacing the hallway and sipping coffee. They tried to overhear what they could, but Fryman and Avion spoke in low, inaudible tones.

At one point, the psychologist stepped outside to ask Mick for some more coffee. Fryman gave no indication how the interview was proceeding.

Then, nearly two hours into the interview, all hell broke loose. The two detectives heard a loud crash followed by a man screaming for help. It was Sam Fryman. Millian rushed in, followed by Bruin. Turgell ran toward the sergeant's desk at the front of the office to get help.

Inside the interrogation room, Avion had pulled Sam Fryman out of his chair and thrown him across the table. Now, he was standing over the terrified psychologist, pummeling him on the back with his fists. Fryman was face down on the table, unable to defend himself, screaming and flailing his arms.

Millian and Bruin raced around opposite ends of the table and yanked Avion away, spinning him around and pinning his face to the wall. Together, they forced his arms behind his back. Mick snapped a pair of handcuffs across his thick wrists and jammed them to the tightest position he could manage. By this time, the

interrogation room was in utter chaos, with both men screaming —
one in terror, the other in anger. Outside, in the hallway, Bruin
could hear the sounds of men running toward them, yelling
instructions to each other.

As Millian got the cuffs on Avion and secured them, two
SRSO officers, who had been at the front of the office, raced into
the room. On their heels was Cindy Turgell. Together, the four
men forced Avion to the far corner of the room. They slammed
him seat-first onto the floor, facing the center of the room. Turgell
went to the head of the table to attend to Fryman.

"What happened here, Frank?" Bruin yelled. "What the hell is
going on? What did you do that for?"

"Fuck you!" the prisoner spat. "Fuck you!"

Millian pushed his way by his partner and cocked his right
fist, threatening to take out his own vengeance. Manny quickly
grabbed him by the arm and spun him around. "Jesus, Mick!
Enough!" He gave Millian a shove that sent him back several feet.

"All right, Frank, calm down," Bruin ordered, turning to face
the man on the floor.

"I'm not Frank, you asshole!" The prisoner's face was
distorted and crimson. "I want a goddamn attorney, *now*! I'm not
Frank anybody!"

Bruin took a few steps back and leaned against the table,
wiping the sweat from his forehead. "You're not Frank?" he asked.
"You're not Frank?"

The big man on the floor said nothing. He just sat there, red-faced, wearing a scaly, tight smile.

Turgell reached across the table and grabbed Bruin's arm. "Manny, he's all right," she said, gesturing toward Fryman. Bruin turned to see Fryman struggling to climb off the table and right himself. He had a large abrasion across his right cheek from where his face had slammed against the tabletop. Otherwise, he seemed relatively intact, although obviously still frightened.

"All right," Bruin yelped. He turned to the two SRSO officers. "Let's get his ass out of here! Arrest him for assault."

"I want an attorney!" Avion screamed. "I want an attorney now! Fuck you all!"

One of the sheriff's officers began to read Avion his rights, struggling to be heard over his protestations. When he had finished, the two officers grabbed Avion by the arms, wrestled him to his feet, and pushed him out of the room. They dragged their prisoner past the sergeant's desk, kicking and screaming all the way, out to an SRSO vehicle, and sped him off to the county jail for booking.

Inside the interrogation room, Turgell helped Sam Fryman into the closest chair and brought him a cup of water. He drank it down in a single breath and slowly began to reorient himself. Out of shape and breathless, the psychologist took several minutes to regain his composure. In the end, though, he seemed little the worse for his ordeal.

Bruin righted one of the overturned chairs and slid it to Fryman. Apparently not yet ready to face his partner, Millian was keeping himself occupied with straightening up the interrogation room and collecting the photographs that were strewn across the floor.

"Sam, are you okay?" Bruin asked gently. "You need some medical attention?"

"I'm all right, Detective. I'll be fine..." He touched his cheek and winced.

"What happened here, Sam? What caused all this?"

"It was one of the photos... Where are the photos?" Fryman replied, scanning the room.

Bruin turned toward Millian with an inquisitive look, also searching for the photos. Mick had already gathered them from the floor and placed them in a stack at the far end of the table. He handed the photos to Manny without saying a word. Bruin pushed the stack toward Fryman.

The psychologist quickly began to leaf through the photographs. After a few seconds, he stopped, realigned the stack, and handed them back to Bruin.

"It's the one on the top, Detective. When your suspect saw that photograph, he went crazy. He reached across the table, grabbed me by the shirt, and slammed my face down onto the table."

Manny looked at the photograph on the top of the stack. It was a picture of Byron Avion and a very young girl. She was naked, except for a pair of white panties, and held her hand toward the camera. He was completely naked, half facing her, half facing the camera. They stood together, close enough to be touching, by the side of a bed. In Avion's hand was the black hood.

Off the Streets

Darren Edwin Hare, the District Attorney for Sonoma County, knew his way around the local political and legal arenas. In his early sixties, Hare had seen it all, or at least everything this semi-rural community had to offer. He was a classic "law and order" prosecutor, whose kindly, manicured presence belied his tough courtroom tactics and tenacity for detail. Hare was exceptionally intelligent, articulate, and capable of striking a deal when he sensed it was in the best interest of his mission. He was the quintessential image of a gentleman and a fine lawyer, who had become an inseparable part of County legal life during his thirty years of service. Most important to the SCCID, Hare was a staunch supporter of local law enforcement.

Much to Bruin's delight, Darren Hare agreed to support each of the initial charges brought against Byron Avion, despite the fact that some of them were, at best, tenuous. The SCCID and SRSO had come together to charge the suspect with two counts of assault, battery, battery against a peace officer, resisting arrest, threats against a peace officer, exploitation of a minor, and lewd and lascivious conduct in the presence of a minor. At least three of the charges were felonies that, should they eventually stick, would deliver hard time. The SCCID was trying to put together yet another case that would support an even more serious felony: child molestation. Much of this legal posturing was clearly stretching the realities of what would actually work in a courtroom. Nonetheless, everyone involved in the Avion case, including Darren Hare, was willing to give it a try. It was the legal equivalent of throwing manure against the barn door to see how much would stick. Bruin had convinced Hare that the defendant was an exceptionally dangerous man, especially around young girls, and that was all the District Attorney needed to hear. Hare promised to take Avion down — and hard.

Avion's first encounter with the Sonoma County Superior Court system was less than a stellar event for the defendant. He had been granted a court-appointed attorney based on his claim that he was indigent and unable to secure the services of his own lawyer. The prisoner had been unable to contact his only close relative, Jacqueline, for assistance — monetary, legal, or otherwise. In truth, she had refused to take his calls. Now, Avion was left with what the local legal system had to offer, which was not much.

At his arraignment, the long list of charges against Byron Avion was read with appropriate solemnity while the defendant's court-appointed counsel, a middle-age tax attorney hastily summoned by the judge, remained seated, silent, and disinterested. With his customary bravado and bellowing courtroom voice, Hare demanded that a bail of $100,000 be imposed, given the serious nature of the charges and his opinion that the defendant posed a flight risk. Avion's attorney said nothing. Judge Wilmer Brigton, well into his seventies and devoid of a sense of humor, quickly approved Hare's request. Avion's preliminary hearing was set for the third week in September 1974, with no objection from either side.

At the end of the nine-minute arraignment, Avion's attorney spoke for the first time, asking to be removed from the case, due to calendar conflicts that would make it impossible for him to continue. Without a question, Brigton approved the request, sending Avion back to the SRSO jail with no attorney and little idea about what had just transpired. Throughout the proceeding, the defendant had not uttered a word. He had not raised his eyes to look at the judge or anyone else. He had not spoken to his court-appointed attorney, nor had the lawyer spoken to him. It was, by all accounts, a strange piece of history, witnessed by no one from the press and only two law enforcement officers: Millian and Bruin.

There was no possibility for Avion to post bail, so he waited in an SRSO cell for two days until the court appointed a second attorney. Avion's new lawyer, a woman in her late twenties named Berta Baily, had never tried a criminal case before. Her special interest was civil litigation. She was young, inexperienced, and clearly over her head. Nevertheless, her number came up, and Judge Brigton made it clear that she would proceed with the case.

He was not about to let a second attorney slip away. Besides that, Berta Baily was not a fishing buddy like Avion's first lawyer, and that was a fact the Judge gave serious consideration.

In the days following his arrest, Avion's behavior continued to be erratic, although not physically violent. From the first, the SRSO jail personnel considered him a threat, based largely on his propensity for screaming at the top of his lungs whenever an SRSO officer came into view. The big man was given a cell by himself, off in the corner of a block that was largely vacant, except for the usual Saturday night drunks. Avion received no personal visitors, but only members of the investigation team, attorneys from both sides, and two psychologists, including Sam Fryman and a second doctor, Ellen Richard, who was working *pro bono* on behalf of Avion's lawyer. It seemed that Berta Baily had friends too, although they were clearly not as influential or well-connected.

The day after Avion's arrest, Bill Calley went to Jacqueline's house to tell her what had happened, just as he had promised. With him was Sam Fryman. At first, Mrs. Avion was reluctant to speak to Fryman, certain that his motives were not in her best interest. It took Bill more than an hour of patient prodding to convince her that Fryman could be trusted. Fryman told her he needed to learn why her son insisted that he was "Frank Avion" and completely rejected anything to do with Byron. He promised to protect her confidentiality.

The answers did not come easily to Jacqueline Avion. Her two visitors stayed nearly four hours before Fryman was convinced he had learned all that he could. Jacqueline would fall silent for long periods, fighting back tears, considering just how far she should go with her explanations. In the end, the psychologist was convinced that she had kept a good deal to herself. But she had also shared enough background to give him a start toward some kind of a diagnosis. Now, after meeting Jacqueline, Fryman also found himself deeply caught up in the case. Whatever was going on in the big man's mind, the psychologist wanted to reach out and make it his own.

As the hours wore on, Jacqueline's disjointed and often halting story began to take some shape. By the time Byron had entered high school, Jacqueline was worried that her son may be suffering from some significant psychological problems, although she never took any action to find out for sure. She said she was so concerned about her son's deteriorating condition that she minimized her contact with Byron, even though they lived in the same house. Jacqueline was terrified of her son, even though he had never attacked her physically and had rarely raised his voice to her. What scared her was his erratic, inexplicable behavior. What Jacqueline saw in her son was the same kind of bizarre, unpredictable behavior that her husband, Frank, had begun to exhibit shortly after their marriage.

Fryman pushed Jacqueline as gently as he could to provide him with a better explanation. Despite his practiced cajoling, she remained deliberately vague, although she did give the psychologist a few tidbits. Both her husband and Byron would sometimes refer to themselves as "different individuals." Frank had developed the habit of referring to himself as "George G," while Byron preferred "Frank." According to Jacqueline's rather convoluted profile, George G was arrogant, sexually demanding, and sometimes physically violent, the polar opposite of the distant, indifferent individual that she had married. Unlike Frank, George G hated his army existence, found excuses to avoid any kind of work around the house, and spent his idle time verbally abusing both Jacqueline and their son. Also, George G was a drunkard, while Frank never touched the stuff.

Thankfully, said Jacqueline, George G was not a frequent visitor. At first, his appearances were rare. By the time the Avions arrived at the Presidio, however, they increased to once or twice a month. When pressed on the point, Jacqueline insisted that her husband never drank, used no drugs, and was otherwise a "wonderful man." She had no explanation for the "George G" personality and no understanding of the name itself. Despite Fryman's repeated attempts to learn more, Jacqueline would not discuss any additional details. She had no idea what this strange, alternate personality meant and when it first arose. Fryman concluded that what Mrs. Avion had discussed with him was truthful. It was what she omitted that troubled him.

As to her son, "Frank" had appeared shortly after her husband's death, as far as she could recall. For some time, Jacqueline assumed that her son simply missed his father and was trying to keep his memory alive by assuming his name. But Frank and Byron were very different individuals. Byron was typically sullen, prone to outbursts of anger and cruelty, and wanted nothing more than to be left alone. Like his father, Byron was virtually wordless around people. Frank, on the other hand, was passive, accommodating, frequently talkative, and emotionally needy, usually to the point that Jacqueline actively avoided him. Mrs. Avion found herself either terrified of the unpredictable Byron or smothered by the ever-present "Frank." Either way, all she wanted from life was to be free of her son, especially after she had escaped any more years with her husband by his untimely, but not unwelcome, death.

The time with Jacqueline Avion was enough to convince Fryman that Byron was a man with significant psychological problems, but he wasn't sure about their nature or genesis. Fryman also came away with a gnawing distaste for Jacqueline, stemming from her unwillingness to be completely open with him and her disdain for her dead husband and incarcerated son. Nonetheless, he also felt a certain compassion. Caught between two impossible men, she had probably done the best that she could to retain her own sanity, escaping into her own world of fantasy and indifference. Now that her son had been arrested and jailed, Jacqueline Avion wanted nothing more to do with him. Her highest hope was that he would somehow just disappear from her life — for good.

Calley's reaction was very different than Fryman's. He felt the inescapable pull of a woman who had lost every emotional battle in her life and now wanted nothing more than to regain the ability to feel something positive. He understood the intensity of her pain and her unwillingness to examine ancient wounds within the cold analysis of a psychologist. By the very nature of his profession, Fryman was indifferent and detached — all too reminiscent of her late husband.

During the weeks between Avion's arraignment and his preliminary hearing, the defendant found himself in the center of a maelstrom of legal maneuvering, psychological assessments, and two carefully structured but disappointing interrogations with Manny Bruin and Mick Millian. As the time approached for the preliminary hearing, Berta Baily, Avion's hard-working, ill-prepared counsel, requested a one-week postponement, claiming that she needed more time to prepare her case based on the complex and unexpected findings of the two psychologists. Much to her relief, Darren Hare did not object and Judge Brigton granted her request. The District Attorney also had some problems with what the psychologists had turned up. Moreover, he was beginning to think in terms of a deal, but he needed a little time to work out the details and present them to Baily.

The two psychologists, Fryman and Richard, agreed on one thing: Byron Avion was definitely not a well man. However, they disagreed on almost everything else, including just how ill he was and how to formalize a diagnosis. From Fryman's point of view, Avion suffered from a significant personality disorder and extreme paranoia. He believed that the suspect was potentially violent and even capable of murder, under the right set of circumstances. Fryman also thought it was possible that Avion's use of the "Frank" persona was a ruse, which he used to manipulate others and avoid direct responsibility for his own actions.

Predictably, Ellen Richard had a different take. She was convinced that Avion suffered from Multiple Personality Disorder, a rare and debilitating psychological illness in which two or more different personalities coexist independently within a single individual. In essence, Richard believed that "Frank" and Byron were two distinct individuals who were unaware of each other. This, she concluded, led to the likelihood that Avion might meet the legal definition of insanity. She was quick to concede that Byron Avion, not "Frank," was capable of violence, but was reluctant to include murder as a possibility. It was clear to Hare that Avion's attorney was working up an insanity defense.

Throughout the weeks of interviews and psychological assessments, Avion seemed to fluctuate between the passive, generally cooperative "Frank," and Byron's abrasive, threatening, and distasteful personality. As far as Fryman was concerned, these episodes seemed more staged than genuine, although he could not be sure that Avion was really in control of the changes. Richard read these fluctuations as further proof of Multiple Personality Disorder, although she admitted that she had never personally encountered a case of MPD in her twelve years of practice. Neither had Sam Fryman.

All of this uncertainty led to a good deal of posturing on both sides. The opinions of Fryman and Richard were also a point of frustration for Bruin and Millian, who saw the possibility of an insanity defense allowing their suspect to walk away from his crimes. As the date for Avion's preliminary hearing drew closer, Baily began talking like a lawyer who was convinced that her client would never be found guilty of a significant crime because of his "obviously severe and debilitating psychological state of mind." To Hare, this sounded like inexperienced bravado designed to cover up a good deal of uncertainty, so he simply gave no indication of his strategy. To all outward appearances, the District Attorney was more than ready to take Baily's client to the mat. Secretly, he had already laid out another plan.

Two days before the scheduled date of Avion's preliminary meeting, Hare arranged for a meeting with Baily and Bruin to discuss "a few, perhaps insignificant details of the case that should be cleared up before we get to court." The two attorneys agreed to meet in a conference room at the Sonoma County Superior Court building. It was this meeting that changed the course of Byron Avion's life and essentially closed the Highway 101 Murder investigation.

Darren Hare had prepared a simple proposition. He would allow Byron Avion to plead "no contest" to the sexually related charges and agree to drop all assault and battery charges so long as Baily's client would agree to voluntary institutionalization on psychiatric grounds, based on the written report of Sam Fryman to the Sonoma County Superior Court. Hare would even allow Baily to present Ellen Richard's findings as part of the presentation to Judge Brigton, to ensure that both sides of the matter were heard. If Baily and her client did not agree to this offer, Hare would proceed with the preliminary hearing and subsequent trial without any other offers to negotiate. In addition, he would attempt to bring a more serious charge of child molestation, and the attorneys would not meet again outside the courtroom. And if Baily was interested in the compromise, she would have to agree by midnight or the whole thing was off.

Berta Baily was stunned, and more than a little angry. Hare had essentially admitted that her client was in need of psychiatric help and he was apparently ready to accede to that point in court. Yet he was obviously just as prepared to throw the concept away and go to a full trial, which included a number of charges that could end in disaster for her client. In the worst-case scenario, should Hare prevail on all or most of the charges, Avion would likely never see the light of day.

Baily demanded to know how Hare could so easily take two opposing points of view. His answer was understated and to the point. Hare wanted Avion off the streets and out of town, any way he could arrange it. It was obvious to both lawyers that he had enough of a case to get some prison time. But that was not enough for the DA. What he really wanted was for Avion to disappear from Santa Rosa. Since Baily was convinced that her client needed long-term psychological help, this was her chance to make that happen.

Baily argued with the older lawyer for some time, mostly on philosophical grounds, to reach a better compromise. But Hare was firm. Make up your mind and make it up by midnight. Here's my card. My home number is on the back. If I hear from you, fine. If not, I'll see you in court. She had no choice but to present the offer to her client.

Coming away from the meeting, Bruin fluctuated between ecstasy and frustration. He liked Hare's approach — and he agreed with it. It was much better to have Avion off the streets, one way or the other. Yet, Hare's solution to the problem would probably leave the Highway 101 investigation out in the cold. It might well kill the investigation completely, unless the murders continued or some new evidence turned up. From Manny's point of view, neither eventuality was likely. He was absolutely sure that the SCCID had gathered all the evidence that it could. There were no new leads, no witnesses, and no tips to follow. Without a confession from Avion, the case was going nowhere. Bruin was also convinced that Avion was the man who had claimed the lives of seven young women. But it was something he knew that he could never prove; and he promised himself that he would not speak about it in public.

If Avion voluntarily agreed to institutionalization, especially based on the findings of Fryman and Richard, it would mean that he could be incarcerated for an indefinite period of time. He would only be released after a three-person board of medical professionals deemed him well enough, and safe enough, to return to society. Given what Fryman and Richard had concluded, and the fact that the medical board would be exceptionally careful in a case like Avion's, the likelihood that he would be released in the near future was almost nonexistent. From Bruin's point of view, that was the good news. But there was a dark side.

During his institutionalization, Avion would almost certainly be out of Bruin's reach. There would be no opportunity for the SCCID to continue to interrogate him, unless something startling turned up in the case. Even more troubling to Bruin was his uncertainty about Avion himself. What if the detective had been wrong about his suspect and the killings continued? If that happened, all hell would break loose and everyone involved in the case would instantly become a political liability. In effect, the

SCCID would be hung out to dry, with Bruin and Millian in the lead.

If Avion agreed to the deal and there were no more killings, the SCCID could still face difficult times. If the defendant refused the deal and went to trial, there was a risk that Avion could be back on the streets much too soon for Bruin's comfort. If not, there was a strong possibility that Bruin's biggest case would never be closed. It would be Avion himself who would determine the outcome to the most important investigation of Bruin's career.

In a rare act of concession to circumstances, Manny decided to take the rest of the afternoon off and spend some time at home, alone. He had had enough of worrying about possibilities. Hare agreed to call him as soon as he heard something. On his way out of the office, Manny left a brief, handwritten message for Millian, giving him an outline of what had happened at the meeting and promising to call him with all the news as soon as it broke. Then he headed home to wait.

That evening, an hour after staring at a dinner he couldn't eat, Bruin received the call. Hare told him that Avion had agreed to the deal. A formalized memorandum had been hastily prepared by the two attorneys, and Baily had presented it to Avion in his cell. The prisoner signed it without making any changes. All that remained was to present the agreement to Judge Brigton, and the case against Byron Avion would be officially closed.

Manny thanked Hare and hung up the phone, telling him that they could talk more about the case tomorrow. He immediately called Millian to give him the news. Mick was uncharacteristically quiet, saying only that he never expected the case would end this way. Still, Mick seemed happy enough that his nemesis would finally be off the streets, even if it was for an indeterminate period. Bruin grumbled his agreement and went off to do something he rarely did — get drunk.

Millian's first move was to call Bill Calley and give him the details. Bill promised to go over to Mrs. Avion's house the next morning to tell her in person. He would be sure to arrive early — he wanted to be the first to tell her. After making the call, in the solitude of his apartment, Mick settled down for the evening with a bottle of his own.

September 22, 1974
Jacqueline Avion's House

Mrs. Avion wrapped her thin arm around Calley's and walked him through the darkened living room to the couch. She was dressed in a long, thickly quilted housecoat decorated with gaudy, oversized white lilies. The ensemble was completed by her standard low, flat loafers and rolled white socks. As Jacqueline sat down next to Bill on the couch, she let out a long sigh.

"You have some news about Byron?" she asked, her eyes nervously wandering.

"Yes, Mrs. Avion. Your son has agreed to voluntarily commit himself to a hospital for psychiatric help." He watched her profile in the dimness. "That means that he won't be going to jail. He'll go to a hospital, although he'll still be in detention."

"What does that *really* mean?" she whispered. "That he'll go to an asylum?"

"From what Mick Millian tells me, it means that he'll be institutionalized and get the help he needs. It's like an asylum, yes, but he'll get help and he won't be able to leave."

"For how long?"

"Until the doctors say that he's well. No one can tell how long. Mick thinks it will be a long time. The truth is... well, no one really knows."

Jacqueline stood and began pacing slowly in front of the couch, back and forth across the patterned rug, rubbing her eyes and shaking her head. Even in the semidarkness, Calley could see that her expression was drawn and concerned.

"He will *never* be well, Mr. Calley..." she droned. "That will never happen."

Bill said nothing.

"He may get out someday, Mr. Calley. Isn't that correct? He *can* get out, correct?"

"Yes. When the doctors say he is well enough, he can get out."

"He will never get better, but he may very well get out someday..." her voice trailed off.

"I don't think they'll let him out if he's not better," Calley offered. "I don't think they'll do that, Mrs. Avion."

"Oh yes they will!" she shot back. "They're not as smart as Byron, whoever they are. He'll fool them, just like he's fooled everyone but me!" Jacqueline stopped and stood in front of him, looking down at his eyes. Her face was set but still gentle.

"Mr. Calley, you have been a big help to me. You've shown me kindness and understanding. You could have treated me much differently, but you did not. I appreciate that and I will always remember it. Byron is *my* problem, not yours. If, or when, he is released from that facility, I will have to deal with it. I *will* deal with him. Now, I don't mean to be offensive, but I must ask you to not contact me again. If we are to ever talk or meet again, it must be on my terms and my terms alone."

Calley was stunned. He slid to his left and stood up, turning to face her.

"I don't understand..."

"That's all right." She reached out to stroke his arm. "You will understand later, Mr. Calley. For now, please, please just do what I ask." Her voice was soft, barely a whisper, but determined.

"But... don't you want to know where Byron will be... don't you want..."

"No," she said firmly. "I know everything that I need to know. I want you to go now. Go home to your family. Go home to your own life. I'll get in touch with you when it's the right time."

Mrs. Avion stepped toward him and again wrapped her arm around his. With a resolute pull, she led him to the front door and yanked it open with her free hand. A final nudge sent him across the threshold. He turned, searching for something to say, his eyes pleading for some kind of explanation. She raised her hand and placed two fingers across his mouth. Her hand lingered for a few seconds, her bony fingers barely caressing his lips. Then, without a word, she stepped back from the threshold and closed the door.

Cold Case

"Well, guys, now that the crowds have thinned out, maybe we can get down to some serious drinking! We've got to get this party *on the move!*" Cindy Turgell delivered three tall, iced whiskeys. Millian flashed her a crooked, drunken smile and put a stranglehold on the glass, just as it settled on the table. He tried to focus on the rest of the dining area, searching for remaining guests with familiar faces. But his eyesight ended in a blur at his fingertips.

"Oh, man..." Bruin grumbled. He patted his stomach, and rolled his eyes. "I don't know, Cindy... I think I've had enough."

Turgell settled into her chair and pulled it up tight against the table, apparently unaffected by the hours of eating and drinking at Fionelli's Italian Restaurant. She worked her hand through a maze of dirty glasses, unused silverware, and discarded bread to slap the back of his hand.

"C'mon, Manny, you're a sergeant now! You should be ripping this place apart! Show us some leadership! All your friends are here... er, were here..." She looked around the nearly vacant restaurant that once held four-dozen SCCID and SRSO partygoers. "It was a hell of a dinner... a hell of a good time. Now, you're sitting here with a stick up your ass! Damn!" She dropped her head and feigned utter frustration.

Bruin chuckled, and looked at his partner. Millian's face was lost in the rim of his whiskey glass, and his eyes were crossed. Bruin decided not to bother him.

"I'm sorry, Cindy," Manny apologized. "I had a heck of a good time, believe me. It was great... you all doing this for me. I appreciate it. Truly"

Cindy smiled politely, gave a passing nod, and put the glass to her lips. She took a slow, easy sip, keeping her eyes on Bruin. Then she set the drink down and cocked her head.

"Yeah, so, what is it, Mick? Where are you, because you're not here with the rest of us? Where are you?"

He shook his head and looked down.

"Avion?" she asked.

"Fuck yeah!" Millian slurred, slamming his empty glass. "Avion! It's always Avion... Jesus!"

By the time of Manny Bruin's promotion to Sergeant in April 1975, Byron Avion had been a guest of the Wildwood State Hospital in eastern Sonoma County for more than six months. Thankfully, the Highway 101 Murders had come to an end, although one of the presumed victims, Kim Kantell, was still listed as a missing person. The small SCCID task force had been disbanded and sent back to their regular assignments. Although the case remained officially open, it received no play in the press and was generally ignored by the political powers of Santa Rosa. For all but the families and friends of the victims, and those close to the investigation, the murders had already become a piece of unsavory local history that was best forgotten. As to tips and leads, Bruin had none. He couldn't even remember when he had last heard a decent rumor.

The talk around town, spawned mostly by a renegade reporter for the Santa Rosa *Journal*, was that the girls and women were claimed by a serial killer who had passed through the area and moved on. Years later, in a highly speculative retrospective, that same reporter would give the killer a name: Ted Bundy. This was clearly the stuff of urban legends and, like many legends, it was widely accepted. However, neither Bruin nor Millian would give it credence. They knew better. Their most important case had gone cold, right in front of their eyes. With each passing week, they knew less and worried more. It was becoming obvious that the murder investigation would never be solved — at least not officially.

In San Francisco, the Zodiac investigation had also ground to a halt. The most notorious fugitive serial killer in Bay Area history had not surfaced in some time. There had been no more letters to the San Francisco *Chronicle*. There were no leads worth pursuing, and the tip line had long ago run dry. Life in the Bay Area had mostly returned to normal, and Zodiac seemed more like a bad dream than a man who had paralyzed a huge metropolitan area.

Sam Lionell, who once directed a cast of hundreds, found himself in charge of three detectives who only worked on the case part-time. Only Lionell continued to believe that his man was out there somewhere. It seemed like everyone else just wanted to forget it, just like the Highway 101 Murders up north. The parallels between the two cases were subtle but, for Manny Bruin, persistent and annoying. He couldn't shake the feeling that the two series of crimes were connected.

At the Wildwood State Hospital, Byron Avion had settled into a bizarre, lifeless routine. The facility was located at the farthest northeastern corner of Sonoma County, well isolated from any significant town, perched on a high hill overlooking open federal land on three sides. A passerby on the country road below couldn't help but view the place as idyllic and tranquil. From a mile away, the facility looked like a rambling, one-story stucco estate that overlooked hundreds of lush, untouched acres of rolling grasslands. Inside the walls, it was a much different story. Overcrowded, understaffed, perpetually noisy, and sometimes dangerous, the facility housed 250 inmate-patients who were often left to fend for themselves, controlled by a staff of only 40 employees. It was a place whose existence no one on the outside wanted to recognize, with a population of forgotten and discarded patients, and a staff that was demoralized, outnumbered, and overworked.

Although there were state-approved protocols for patient treatment, their effectiveness was minimal. Most patients were destined to spend their lives behind the facility walls, unless they were somehow able to pull themselves out of their psychological illnesses and prove it to a skeptical, disinterested three-person review board. For the staff at Wildwood, the central issue was not treatment but patient control, driven by their own fears and concerns for safety.

Immediately after his arrival at Wildwood, Byron Avion was put on a regimen of antidepressants and sedatives, more to enhance the staff's ability to manage his angry outbursts than as a form of treatment. By the end of the first month, he had received an official diagnosis that was forwarded to Sam Fryman and the SCCID: Avion was said to be suffering from schizophrenia, paranoia, and depression. There was no evidence of Multiple Personality Disorder and the patient had not once referred to himself as "Frank" or any other alternate personality. The staff and attending psychiatrist considered him potentially dangerous. His prognosis for even a partial recovery was bleak. By all accounts, Avion was an ideal candidate for a lifetime sentence at Wildwood, which greatly pleased Bruin and Millian. Fryman, however, was skeptical. He had little faith in the Wildwood protocols, and even less regard for the medical staff that carried them out. From Fryman's point of view, these kind of snap diagnoses were mostly motivated by a need to waddle through bureaucratic hoops.

Because Avion persisted in his habit of screaming at anyone in authority, he was initially locked in his room for most of the day, usually under sedation. In the early evening, Avion was sedated again, so that he would sleep through the night and not bother anyone. As to any other psychiatric treatment, the patient was required to attend a group session with seven male sex offenders three times a week. These sessions were scheduled for two hours but usually adjourned early when they became too difficult to control. Avion also received individual therapy for one hour, twice a week, from Dr. Richard Bennington, one of Wildwood's practicing administrators and the man who diagnosed his illnesses when he arrived.

Heavily medicated and considered hostile by everyone who came into contact with him, Avion spent most of his waking hours in a semi-conscious stupor in his six- by eleven-foot room, located in a section of the facility that housed violent sex offenders. For the first two months, the new arrival was not allowed to interact with other patients in the day room, although that restriction was later lifted as his behavior became more predictable and controlled. Eventually, he was even allowed to stroll alone in the fenced courtyard for up to an hour, under the close eye of a custodian.

As Manny Bruin was celebrating his promotion in April 1975, Avion's personal contact record at Wildwood indicated that he had received no outside visitors since his arrival. He had made no requests to place a telephone call, nor had he received any calls, and he had written no letters or postcards. He had received no mail. No official inquiries had been made from any outside agency on his behalf. Beyond the walls of the psychiatric facility, Avion had become a non-entity, except for those who had remained close to the victims of the Highway 101 Murderer — and, of course, his pursuers.

April 1978
A Last Hurrah

Three years had slipped away since Manny Bruin's promotion. These were quiet, comfortable days in Sonoma County. Across the rest of the nation, matters were not so tranquil.

In September 1975, publishing heiress Patty Hearst, who was kidnapped the previous year by a militant group calling itself the Symbionese Liberation Army, was captured by the FBI. The media went wild, plastering the young woman's face everywhere and speculating about her real role in the gruesome events that preceded her arrest. Everyone was amazed, and everyone had an opinion. Was Patty a spoiled rich girl, who had been voluntarily transformed into a militant criminal, or was this a classic case of the Stockholm Syndrome? The following year, at the height of the U.S. bicentennial, David Berkowitz, the Son of Sam serial killer, began his murderous rampage in New York. The killings would last for a year before Berkowitz was finally caught. Like Patty Hearst before him, Berkowitz's face would become a familiar image across America. For Santa Rosans, it was all too reminiscent of their own brush with serial murder.

For those Sonoma County citizens who clung to the lighter side of life, the Santa Rosa *Journal* had some exciting front-page headlines in 1978. The racing season witnessed a combination of man and beast that proved hard to forget — with some local connections. "Affirmed" won horse racing's Triple Crown that year. On board was a seventeen-year-old jockey, Steve Cauthen. It was rumored in town, thanks to the *Journal*, that Affirmed had once worked out on a farm somewhere east of the city center. Predictably, the name of the farm and the source of the story remained anonymous.

That same year, Santa Rosa found itself in the midst of a mini-growth spurt, with the town population now teetering at 80,000. Outside the Santa Rosa limits, especially to the east, the once barren, rolling hills were beginning to show signs of organized life with the construction of a few expensive, sprawling ranch homes. To those who had spent many years in the area, it was clear that the Holsteins that once freely roamed those hills were beginning to experience unparalleled competition of a two-legged variety. This did not come as good news to the local citizenry and was regularly the topic of grumbling editorials in the Santa Rosa *Journal* that year.

At the SCCID office, the hand of time had given Manny Bruin an unexpected, unwelcome slap. He had gained nearly twenty-five pounds since his promotion and now found himself interred in endless and seemingly pointless administrative tasks. It was a rare day when the sergeant would find himself out on the streets, doing what he did best. To make matters worse, his friend and partner, Mick Millian, seemed better than ever. Millian had given up drinking in late 1975, and looked trim, energetic, and pleased with life — quite a change from his days of chasing Byron Avion. He was also able to spend most of his time on investigative work in the field, which, as with Bruin, had always been his favorite pursuit.

District Attorney Hare retired in 1977, amidst an outpouring of accolades and overt acts of sentimentality. Interestingly, he never again stepped inside a courtroom after the Byron Avion arraignment. Things had been that good in town for that long, and his waning years were spent muddling through paperwork and chatting with local political figures. Unfortunately, Hare's successor, who was half his age, would prove to possess only half his wits.

Cindy Turgell found herself relegated to the usual questionable deaths, although very few of them turned out to be wrongful. By 1978, she was spending a good deal of time at the local university, passing on her knowledge and skills in a series of graduate courses that were among the most popular on campus. As with Millian, the years had treated her well. She was an ageless soul.

Bill Calley continued to work in the court system and as a volunteer for the American Red Cross and the Santa Rosa Little League. Jacqueline Avion never contacted Calley, and he remained true to his word to avoid contacting her. Rumor had it that Jacqueline was out of the country more often than not. When Bill would occasionally drive by her house, he would always find the living room drapes tightly drawn, no sign of life, except for the hired gardener who made his weekly appearance.

Once each year, Byron Avion received a formal psychiatric evaluation from the powers at Wildwood. Each year the written results were shared with Sam Fryman, who then passed them on to Manny Bruin for the SCCID files. The bottom line was always familiar, and droll. The patient had not made any significant progress; he continued to suffer from the maladies first presented, although his depression had eased somewhat. Avion was still diagnosed as suffering from schizophrenia and was still subject to significant bouts of paranoia, although they, too, had eased. As usual, the patient's prognosis was poor. He remained isolated from the outside world, with no record of visitors, incoming or outgoing telephone calls, or mail.

The Santa Rosa *Journal* had apparently forgotten about the Highway 101 Murders. The paper carried no retrospectives, no news about the investigation, and no mention of the young victims. The *Journal's* pages were filled with the usual trivia that occupies the attention of a not-so-small-town in the making: uncontrolled growth, fights over building permits, sewer line capacities, and even a growing problem with pollution. Crime was not a hot issue — at least violent crime — but the paper did carry a daily summary of police calls. Those who followed this inside piece couldn't help but notice that it, too, was growing.

Then, in the last week of April 1978, a strange, uncertain wind moved up from the south. It came in the form of a phone call from Sam Lionell to Manny Bruin.

"Manny! Manny, how are you?" Lionell shouted. It had been years since the two men had talked yet the SFPD detective made it sound as if they had been out to dinner the night before.

"Yeah, I'm fine, Sam. Wow... it's been quite a while..." Bruin's voice was guarded.

"Well, that's *my* fault Manny," he admitted. "I've been hung up here with way too much work and not enough time. Everything just kind of slipped away and, well... you know..."

"Sure, I understand. Same story here, for sure. So, Sam, what's going on in the big city? Anything exciting? I haven't heard much about the Zodiac case lately." Manny immediately regretted the question.

"Well... that's true, Manny," came the halting reply. "The fact is... well... the damn case is a fish, my friend. It's as cold as it gets. I'm down to just a few detectives and everyone around here wants me to roll over and give it up. They're talking about sending the case to Sacramento... so the state folks can handle it. They're talking about closing it down completely at the local level."

"I'm sorry to hear that, Sam. That's got to make you feel lousy..."

"Well, yeah, it does..." was the slow, quiet reply. "And... well... that's not the worst of it, Manny. A week ago, the freak wrote another letter to the *Chronicle*."

"You're kidding! Zodiac? He wrote a letter!?"

"Yeah."

"Jesus! I didn't read about it in the paper or anything."

"Yeah, well...we capped it quick, Manny. That's the problem. There are some powerful folks around here who say the letter is a forgery. Now, it's going to appear in the paper in the next two or three days. That's the agreement we have with the *Chronicle*. But... well, this forgery thing is pretty bad for the case... and for me."

"Okay, Sam. I think I understand. How can I help?"

"You probably can't, Manny. I just wanted you to know... and, well, I *do* have one question, then we'll both just have to wait and see what happens."

"Okay, Sam, shoot. What's the question?"

"I just wanted to confirm that your guy, Avion, is still in the wacko house up there."

"Yeah, he's still at Wildwood, Sam."

"Do you ever get to see the visitor reports on him?" Sam asked.

"Yeah, once a year; sometimes twice a year. The guy has no visitors. In fact, no calls, no mail, no nothing. That's the way it's been since he got there."

"Oh, Christ..." Lionell moaned. "That figures. Well, Manny, he was a long shot anyway, wasn't he? I mean, the guy is a freak but I don't think he's the man I've been after all this time."

Manny stayed quiet for several seconds.

"All right, Manny," Sam said, his voice back to chipper. "Listen, I appreciate your help. Anytime I can reciprocate, you just let me know. One of these days, we've got to get together and tell some war stories, right?"

"You bet, Sam. I'd like that," Bruin replied. He was still waiting for the punch line when Lionell let the handset slip back to the cradle.

Three days later, the *Chronicle* carried the last of Zodiac's letters. It had been nearly four years since the killer had surfaced and now he was proclaiming that he had been hovering around the edges of the investigation since its beginning, always in sight but never seen. For some members of the SFPD, along with key politicos in San Francisco, the sudden, unexpected appearance of a

Zodiac letter stretched credibility to the breaking point. Several handwriting experts were immediately called in to examine the document. Some proclaimed it to be the real thing, while others insisted that it was a forgery. In the end, the SFPD refused to beef up its once-substantial Zodiac task force. This final missive, real or forgery, didn't really change things much. No one cared about Zodiac these days, except for Sam Lionell, and he was a solo missionary without a flock. Today, two and a half decades after that last letter appeared, no one can say whether or not it was the genuine article. The fact that both the Highway 101 Murders and the Zodiac case went cold at nearly the same time never made the press, either in Santa Rosa or San Francisco.

One month later, in May, Mick Millian received the best news he could imagine. Bruin had quietly recommended that the detective be promoted to sergeant, two years ahead of his scheduled date to take the exam. The recommendation sailed through every layer above Bruin and came back in record time with nothing but solid support. Millian couldn't believe it. He was sure that he had managed to work his way onto *someone's* shit list after so many years mucking around town. But he was wrong. Millian was a doer and everyone knew it.

On the Saturday after he received the good news, Mick was dragged away to Fionelli's Italian Restaurant, along with thirty other hard-drinking souls from the ranks of the SRSO, SCCID, and even the SRPD. He made an exception that night and got riotously drunk. Turgell was well-tipped but seemed to maneuver across the floor in relative safety. Bruin was in the bag and loving it.

The next day, Millian was at work early with plenty of aspirin and vows of never-again. Bruin stayed home and made no excuses for his absence. Turgell, who had never missed a day at the office, called in sick and became the brunt of some pointed but friendly barbs.

July 1979
Final Uncertainty

1979 was a year of uncertainty, worry, and disappointment across our country. In March, a major accident occurred at a nuclear reactor on Three Mile Island in Pennsylvania. Later that year, 63 Americans were taken hostage at the U.S. embassy in Tehran, Iran, by militant followers of the Ayatollah Khomeini.

In Santa Rosa, the unthinkable happened. The remains of a young woman were found in a remote area east of the city center. The uneasy belief that the town had heard the last of the Highway 101 Murderer was given one last, unexpected blow. To this day, the event remains the most troubling enigma of the entire case.

In the middle of July, late on an intensely hot afternoon, a local rancher, Tim Collins, came across an oversized, threadbare blue laundry bag near the side of the road along the western boundary of his land. The bag had ended up in a narrow, natural crevice, where it was covered by years of brush and soil. Had it not been for a small patch of faded blue cloth sticking up from underneath, Collins might never have seen it

With a good deal of effort and more care than one would have expected, the rancher worked the bag free of the brush and soil. He noticed that it had once been tightly tied around the top with what looked like white nylon rope. Now, the rope was little more than a series of tattered strands that barely held the cloth together. He slipped the strands from the neck of the bag, gently pulled it open, and looked inside. Collins gasped and stumbled backward when he saw what was inside. It was a human skeleton.

The rancher left the bag next to the crevice and made his way back to his pickup truck a half-mile down the road. From there, he raced to his ranch house overlooking the valley and telephoned the SRSO. In turn, they contacted Manny Bruin and Cynthia Turgell. Less than an hour later, the scene of the discovery had been lined off and was swarming with law enforcement and forensic personnel. Remarkably, no one from the Santa Rosa *Journal* made it to the site.

Turgell, among the first to arrive, was reluctant to examine the remains at the dumpsite. She was concerned that disturbing the skeleton in such a non-controlled environment would do irreparable damage to potential forensic evidence. Turgell had the laundry bag and its contents carefully transported to the ME's office in the coroner's wagon. All that she could tell Bruin at the dumpsite was that the remains were several years old. She couldn't tell if they belonged to a man or woman. However, they were clearly too large to belong to a child. Everything else would have to wait for a thorough examination.

Although they didn't discuss the possibilities that afternoon, both Turgell and Bruin believed that these remains belonged to a victim of the Highway 101 Murderer. Even though he had never used a laundry bag before, this victim had been dumped in the killer's favorite area. That alone was enough to set the alarms off for Bruin, who often worried about finding other bodies along this isolated stretch. Both Turgell and Bruin thought that the skeleton would eventually be identified as that of Kim Kantell.

Kantell, a thirteen-year-old, had vanished nearly seven years earlier, in 1972, while hitchhiking south on Highway 101. She disappeared on a chilly December morning and had not been heard from since. The SCCID had listed her as a missing person, but Bruin, Millian, and Turgell were convinced that Kim had been abducted and murdered, probably by the same man who had claimed the other Highway 101 victims. The remains discovered by Tim Collins were located less than a hundred yards from where the body of Leslie Buono was found in 1972.

Back at the Medical Examiner's office, Cindy Turgell placed a call to Dr. Victor Stinesky of San Francisco University. It had been Stinesky who worked with Turgell in 1972 to identify the remains of Mary Spooner and Elaine Calley. Now, she needed his help once again. All Turgell had in her possession was a fragile skeleton, which she was reluctant to remove from the laundry bag that contained it. This kind of situation was definitely in Stinesky's domain, and just the kind of challenge that intrigued him the most. Despite his advanced years, the professor dropped what he was doing and drove the fifty miles from his office.

Turgell and Stinesky worked without a break until two o'clock the next morning. The skeleton in the laundry bag demanded a good deal of care; its long exposure to the elements had rendered it disjointed and partially brittle. Stinesky estimated that the body had been discarded at least five years earlier, perhaps as many as ten. The remains had been fairly well protected from the elements because of its cloth wrapper and its location in the ground. From the anthropologist's point of view, this had been a fortunate set of circumstances, preventing any large predators from scattering or damaging the bones.

It was clear from the position of the skeleton that the victim had been bound, both hand and foot, prior to the time of death. Shredded, deteriorating pieces of white nylon rope were scattered throughout the interior of the bag and on several bones. However, there was nothing else inside the container by which Turgell could identify the remains. The victim had apparently been abandoned without any articles of clothing or personal effects. Once again, as in all the previous cases, there was a complete paucity of forensic evidence.

After several hours of meticulously reconstructing and examining the skeleton, Stinesky came to the conclusion that the victim had been a young female, probably in her late teens, who had never given birth. She stood about five feet, six inches tall. A few strands of auburn hair were recovered from the skull area, which led the anthropologist to conclude that the victim had long, reddish-brown hair. There were no indications how the victim died, and no obvious trauma to the skeleton.

Turgell was stunned at Stinesky's findings. Based on what the professor had determined, the victim in the laundry bag could not have been Kim Kantell. On the date of her disappearance, Kim was only thirteen years old. She stood only five feet tall, and had dark, nearly black hair that was cut very short. Whoever had been murdered and stuffed into the laundry bag was not Kim. It was another, unknown victim — another young woman who had probably been claimed by the Highway 101 Murderer but who had never been reported missing.

Turgell and Stinesky agreed that the only way to make a positive identification was to attempt to match her dental records. Fortunately, the entire skull and jaw had been well-preserved. Stinesky carefully wrapped these in a series of paper bags, which he then placed in a cardboard box. The professor would bring the remains to San Francisco University, where he would give them to the head of the School of Dentistry for an examination the following morning. Once the teeth and jaw were profiled, they would be returned to Turgell. In the meantime, the profile would be used to try to find a match with dental records on file. Unfortunately, that would be a slow, laborious process that could take months. In the meantime, the SCCID would have to work with the meager physical description of the victim that Stinesky had provided.

Despite the ungodly hour, Turgell called Manny Bruin at home to give him the preliminary results of her findings. Like Turgell, Manny was shocked. He had been certain that the victim would prove to be Kim Kantell. Now it was obvious that the Highway 101 Murderer had claimed at least one victim who had not been missed, or at least not reported missing. The tired, angry detective couldn't get back to sleep. At four o'clock, he was pulling to a stop in front of the SCCID office, obsessed with the other unnamed, unknown victims who might lie in the hills east of town.

Within a day of the discovery, the Santa Rosa *Journal* caught wind of the story and was hot on Bruin's trail. With his customary low-key approach, the detective gave away as little information as possible. Naturally, the crucial question was whether or not he believed that this victim had been claimed by the Highway 101 Murderer. Bruin was direct and open on this point. He didn't know, but the preliminary information he received from the ME's office indicated that the remains were several years old. That kind of timing made it a possibility. Because of the condition of the remains, it would be some time before a positive identification was made, so nothing could be ruled in or out. Manny promised to hold a press conference as soon as the SCCID could confirm the identity of the victim and notify the next of kin.

Remarkably, the *Journal* wrote the story almost exactly as Bruin had laid it out. There was no speculation, no criticism of an open, cold case, and no attempt to draw sensational conclusions. In fact, the first two pieces on the grisly find only mentioned the *possibility* that the Highway 101 Murderer was connected with the crime. In effect, Bruin, Millian, and the rest of the SCCID had dodged a major political setback with the local journalists. It seemed that the media, too, had little desire to fuel the painful, unresolved memories of the Highway 101 victims.

In the end, the young victim discovered by Tim Collins was never identified. She matched none of the descriptions of missing persons in Sonoma County or any adjoining county. The combined efforts of the SRSO, SCCID, and a dozen other local agencies failed to find a match to the dental profile. The Santa Rosa *Journal* dropped the story after running only three articles, all within six weeks of the discovery. By winter, all the SCCID was able to learn was that the skeleton in the laundry bag was almost certainly not Kim Kantell.

Then, in December of that year, Bruin received an even bigger shock. Just before Christmas he learned that Byron Avion was about to be set free.

Coming Home

"What!?" Millian screamed. He jumped from his chair and pounded on the table. "This is pure bullshit! How can they release him? What the hell is going on here?"

Manny pushed him on the shoulder, forcing him back into his seat. "Listen, Mick, just *listen* to what Sam has to say, will you? Please, just *sit down*!"

Millian curled his lip into an angry scowl and sat mute, staring at the psychologist.

"Okay, good." Bruin said, sitting back down. "I want to hear this too, Sam. How come Avion's on the way out of there? What's going on?"

Fryman looked around the table at the two detectives and Turgell, taking a moment to decide where to begin. He looked uncertain and embarrassed.

"It's not pleasant, Manny... what's going on here. Avion's not the only one who's going to be released over the next few weeks. It's a matter of politics and economics. Up in Sacramento, they've cut back the funding for state institutions by half. They ordered each facility to rank their patients according to their potential for violence and the progress of their recovery. The bottom line is that the state is flushing the system by half. A lot of the patients —

those they figure are no longer a clear danger — are getting early releases. Avion is one of them."

"That's nuts..." said Turgell. "It doesn't make any sense. Who's to decide which one is dangerous and which one is not? How the hell can bureaucrats decide that kind of thing?"

Fryman nodded but said nothing.

"Isn't there anything we can do about it?" Bruin asked. "We just have to let this happen?"

"That's right, Manny, there's nothing we can do about it. From Wildwood's perspective, Avion is not considered as volatile — as violent — as a lot of the others. They see him as a screamer, not as someone who is physically violent any longer. He made the cut, I'm afraid."

"Oh, man!" Millian spouted, again jumping from his chair. "There's no way I'm going to have that sick fuck running around town! I'll kill the son-of-a-bitch first!"

Mick angrily threw his chair to the floor and stormed out of the room, leaving the others in silence. For a long moment, no one spoke.

"He doesn't mean that," Turgell whispered. "He's just blowing off steam."

"I don't know about that," Manny replied.

1980
A Lousy New Year

The holidays were always depressing for Manny Bruin, even in the best of times. This year, they were indescribable, and it was all because his most important case had gone full circle to nowhere. Byron Avion returned to his mother's house two days after Christmas and there was nothing the SCCID could do about it. He was a free man, declared well by a committee in the state capitol whose real concern was a shrinking budget. Now it was left up to the local jurisdictions to clean up the mess — to deal with the mistakes. Bruin spent the holidays in a depression that seemed endless.

Unlike his partner, Millian fumed and fussed for months on end. He badgered and cajoled everyone in sight, including Bruin, about the unfairness of Avion's release — the unbridled stupidity of letting this man roam the streets once again. Over the ensuing months, the two detectives met several times with the new District Attorney, Mel Vialarri, trying to figure out how far they could go to keep an eye on their suspect. The DA was adamant that Avion be left alone. He was a free man now and he had the same rights as anyone else. The SCCID had no choice but to back off and do nothing. Millian quickly concluded that Vialarri was a man who had little common sense and even less in the way of balls. He decided never to deal with him again.

Throughout the first few months of 1980, Mick spent even more time than usual with Bill Calley, grousing about his nemesis and plotting a hundred ways to keep the man within his sights. At first, Calley listened patiently and tried to console his old friend, but secretly he no longer had the will to be part of any plan to bring Avion down. By summer, Calley had had enough of his friend's obsession and demanded that Millian just let it go, just help him to put the memory of Elaine's death behind him. But Mick couldn't stop himself. Calley began avoiding the detective, finding all kinds of thin excuses to do so.

For the first six months after his release from Wildwood, Byron Avion rarely left his mother's home. Almost immediately, Millian fell back into his old habit of watching the Avion residence in his off-hours, sometimes throughout the night. He had expected to see Avion resume his nighttime journeys, but that never happened. From time to time, the big man would open the front door and stand on the porch by himself, staring out across the driveway. Then he would slip back inside. He would always be dressed in the same way: a white undershirt and black pants, regardless of the weather. Millian never saw his man leave the porch, and he never saw Jacqueline Avion.

In July, Mick inadvertently discovered that Avion had landed a job when the big man's habits suddenly changed. The suspect would leave his home around 7:30 in the morning and walk nearly a mile to the NorSo Discount Store, which was located in a shopping center near the fringe of downtown. He would invariably dress in blue work pants, a cotton shirt of the same color, and heavy boots. Each weekday morning, he would report to the back of the huge facility by eight o'clock and disappear inside. After some discreet checking, Mick learned that Avion had been hired as a stockman, earning minimum wage for loading and unloading pallets of goods as they were delivered to the rear entrance. For a time, Millian tried watching the store, but never learned anything interesting.

Each day, Avion would leave NorSo at 5:30 in the afternoon and walk back to his mother's house, where he would disappear for the night. Millian never saw him interact with another soul. For the rest of that summer and into October, this routine didn't change. As far as Millian could tell, the big man never left his mother's house, unless it was to go to work.

In the last week of October, the SRSO received a telephone call from the manager of NorSo, asking that a deputy be sent to the store right away. The angry, distressed woman on the telephone explained that one of her clerks, an eighteen-year-old, had been threatened by a co-worker, Byron Avion. Within the hour, a young, female deputy was on the scene, taking a report. It seemed that Avion had cornered the young clerk outside the employee lunch area and demanded that they meet somewhere for sex. When she refused, Avion became angry and shoved her against the wall, frightening her but leaving her uninjured. He then stormed out of the building without saying a word.

The SRSO deputy asked to speak to the clerk who had been threatened, but the teenager refused to say anything. In fact, she now denied the entire incident, even though she had reported it to the manager immediately after it happened. Despite the deputy's patient prodding and offers of assistance, the girl remained firm. She simply wasn't going to talk about what had happened. Left without options, the SRSO deputy summarized the events in a brief incident report and filed it away. Word of the event never made it to the SCCID office, and Avion never returned to his job at NorSo after that day. In fact, he never again left his mother's home alive.

December 20, 1980
Sonoma County Medical Examiner's Office

Bruin stood silently at the threshold to Cindy Turgell's office, waiting for her to sense his presence. She was buried in stacks of papers strewn across her desk, working feverishly to find a report that had gone astray. Finally, she realized someone was staring at her.

"Oh, Christ..." she said. "I didn't see you there, Manny, sorry. Come on in." She smiled and pointed to the creaky metal chair on the other side of her desk. He slid inside the office and sat down with a sheepish look on his face.

"Listen, Cindy, I'm really sorry about yesterday... jumping down your throat and storming out like that. I'm sorry." He was having trouble looking her in the eye.

She nodded. "Sure. I understand... it's okay, Manny."

"This thing with Avion has made me crazy, probably just as crazy as Mick. It's just that... well... I don't let it go on the outside, you know. I kind of keep it all inside."

She nodded and let him continue.

"Anyway, it's over now. He's dead and that's that. So, I'm really sorry about the way I behaved. Maybe we can do dinner tonight and talk. Would that be okay with you?"

"Yeah, Manny, fine. Tonight's good for me," she said, reaching across the desk to pat his arm.

"Ok, great. I'll call you up later with a time, after we both clear things up a bit." He waved an arm at the clutter on her desk. "You can give me the report on Avion anytime. I'm not in a hurry anymore. No need to be..."

He stood and began to move toward the door, obviously happier than when he entered.

"Wait a second, Manny," she said in a low tone. "There's something about the Avion report that we should discuss. That's what I wanted to talk to you about yesterday."

He turned around and stepped close to her desk with a worried look on his face. She motioned toward the chair but he shook his head. He would stand.

"Listen, Manny, Avion's death *looked* to be from natural causes..." She waited for him to pick up her meaning.

"Looked?" he echoed, sitting down

"I'm sure that he wasn't alone when he died," Turgell said quietly.

"How do you know that?" the detective asked.

"I found some black fibers in his hair, Manny — also along the side of his face. Something was covering his head and it was made of black cloth. There were also a few stands of long gray hairs on one of his arms and hand. I think they were deposited on the body after death."

"Oh, Christ..." Bruin gasped.

Manny's skin had turned nearly white and he was furiously rubbing his hands together, right over left, left over right. Turgell had a decision to make.

"Listen, Manny, it wasn't Mick, if that's what you're thinking. I mean, the hairs I found couldn't have been his."

"That doesn't mean he wasn't there!" Bruin shot back.

"No... it doesn't," she conceded, "but I don't think it was him." Turgell dropped her head, unwilling to say any more.

"Cindy, what are you going to put in that report? I need to know. What's it going to say? Do we have a problem?"

She sat motionless and silent for several seconds. Then, without looking up, she gave him her decision.

"Byron Avion died of natural causes. He died alone in his basement. It was a good thing, Manny."

May 1981
Bill Calley's Residence

It was a warm, breezy Saturday morning in Santa Rosa, the perfect kind of day to sit on the porch and watch the neighborhood come alive. Calley snuggled himself into an oversized, well-stuffed redwood chair, and stared out across the street, letting the early sun warm his face. He had just begun to drift into a light snooze when he heard his name being called.

"Mr. Calley?" she asked. "Are you Mr. Calley?"

The woman at the bottom of the porch was unfamiliar. Matronly, but well dressed in a gray suit, she wore a serious, determined expression. His first thought was that she was either a lawyer or a Jehovah's Witness. Nonetheless, Calley was never one to turn someone away.

"Yes, I'm Bill Calley," he answered politely. He pushed himself up from the chair and moved to the edge of the porch. "Come on up," he continued, waving her forward.

"No, thanks, Mr. Calley. I have to run. I just wanted you to know that Mrs. Avion died. She died two days ago, in her home."

"Oh..." he replied. "I'm sorry to hear that. I haven't seen her in... well..."

"Yes, I know," the stranger interrupted. "She mentioned you often. She was very fond of you. In fact, she gave me something before she died and I have it with me. It's something she wanted you to have."

Calley's eyes widened. He worked his way down the steps to join her at the foot of the porch.

"This is it," the woman said, holding out a small cardboard box. "This is for you."

Calley reached out to take it. "What is it?" he asked.

"Please read the letter, Mr. Calley. It's on the top. Mrs. Avion wanted to be sure that I told you to read the letter. Will you do that for her?"

"Of course," he answered, "But, I need to..."

The woman in gray shook her head and put a finger to her lips. There was nothing else to say. She turned around and walked briskly down the block, disappearing around the corner.

Calley stood at the foot of the porch, watching her vanish from sight, trying to recollect if he had ever seen her before.

Climbing back up the stairs, he turned the box over in his hands, testing its weight and trying to guess the contents. Then he opened the front door and made his way into the dining room at the back of the house. He placed the box on the table and carefully opened the flaps, revealing a note-sized envelope that had been hand-addressed with his name. He pulled a single, buff-colored page from the unsealed envelope and began to read the shaky, tilting script:

Dear Mr. Calley:

Please forgive me for not contacting you personally for all this time. I am sure, by now, that you understand why I could not. Whatever happened, I certainly did not want you to become involved.

There is nothing we can do for the dead but let them rest. Those young couples, the girls and women, are in my heart and always in my prayers. I hope that you will see your way clear to let my memory rest also, but that must be your decision.

My son was a monster. I have tried to set that right but I was afraid to accept the consequences of my actions, so I said nothing. My only hope was to spend my last few years peacefully, knowing that Byron could do no more harm. Thank God, that happened. He will judge my awful deed. He will know if I have done right or wrong. I cannot say.

I have enclosed a few items that I want you to have. You may do what you want with them. I truly hope that they will help to answer your questions fully. Perhaps they will help you find some ease among all the pain that my son has made you suffer.

You have been in my prayers each day, Mr. Calley. I hope that you will find some time to pray for a very old, very bad woman who tried to make things right in the end.

Sincerely,

Jacqueline Avion

Calley slipped the letter onto the dining room table and reached inside the cardboard box, removing the rectangular object that lay on top. Wrapped in white tissue was the old, faded photograph of Jacqueline Avion and her childhood friend in front of the church. It was still encased in its ornate frame, although it had obviously been years since anyone had given it any care.

Beneath the photograph, Bill found a tightly rolled length of black linen. It had been secured with two stout rubber bands. He pulled the roll from the box, slid the rubber bands off each end, and unfurled the cloth. The piece of material that now lay across his table had been hand-sewn into the form of a black hood. Openings had been carefully cut into the fabric where the eyes, nose, and mouth of a large man would naturally fall. The hood had an extended piece of material sewn onto it, just below the area of the chin or neck. It was rectangular, about a foot in length and nearly as wide. Emblazoned on this extension was a familiar symbol, meticulously sewn in place with what appeared to be white satin.

At the bottom of the box, nudged into a corner, Calley discovered a piece of blue felt that had been folded over and tied with thin white ribbon. He carefully untied the ribbon and set the cloth on the table, unwrapping its folds with deliberate slowness. Inside, he found two pairs of small, gold hoop earrings, just like those the girls had been wearing that last Christmas.

Later that night, long after the others had gone to bed, Bill Calley sat alone, in front of the fire in his living room, watching the last remnants of the black hood as it vanished into smoke and ash. In his hand, he held the four gold hoops. Above him, on the mantel, in a polished and renewed frame, two young girls looked down at him from beyond the door of a forgotten church.

He hadn't noticed it before, but now it seemed as though both of them were smiling — the easy, innocent smiles of those who had finally come home.

Appendix I — Key Individuals

A case as complex and enigmatic as the Highway 101 Murders is bound to generate a large and diverse cast of characters. Here are a few of the most important individuals connected with the investigation:

- **Cathy Alverson,** a 19-year-old student at Santa Rosa Junior College, was the third known victim of the Highway 101 Murderer. She disappeared in March 1972 while hitchhiking along Highway 101 in the area of the college. Her body was later discovered in a dry creek bed near a country road in Sonoma County. Alverson had been bound, strangled with white nylon clothesline, and had her clothes taken by her killer. As with several other victims, one of Alverson's earrings had been removed.

- **Byron Avion** was born in 1934 in Los Angeles. By the early 1970s, he lived in San Francisco, California, but also maintained an apartment in Santa Rosa, where he would spend much of his time. Highly intelligent, resourceful, and manipulative, Avion had no criminal record until the mid-1970s, when he was charged with a variety of crimes, some sexual in nature, and subsequently institutionalized. He died in Santa Rosa in 1980.

- **Berta Baily** was the second court-appointed attorney for Byron Avion following his arrest in 1974. Avion's first court-appointed attorney withdrew from the case at the close of his arraignment in Sonoma County Superior Court.

- **Judge Wilmer Brigton**, Sonoma County Superior Court, was the judge appointed to the Byron Avion case in 1974.

- **Manuel ("Manny") Bruin**, Lieutenant and Chief Homicide Inspector, Sonoma County Criminal Investigations Division

(SCCID). Bruin was actively involved in the Zodiac investigation after the killer's attack on Cecilia Shepherd and Bryan Hartnell on September 27, 1969, at Lake Berryessa in neighboring Napa County. In 1972, while still working on the Zodiac investigation, Bruin was assigned to the Highway 101 Murders case before it was known that a serial killer was active in the area. At the time, Bruin had been a member of the SCCID for nearly five years and had limited experience in working serial homicide cases. He would later be promoted to Sergeant, then Lieutenant, and finally Chief Homicide Investigator for the SCCID.

▪ **Leslie Buono**, thirteen years old, vanished in November 1972. Buono's body was found a few weeks after her disappearance. She was the fifth known victim of the Highway 101 Murderer. She was nude, had suffered a broken neck, and both of her earrings were missing. A piece of white nylon clothesline was discovered near her body.

▪ **Terry Calan,** a twenty-three year old, was abducted along Highway 101 in December 1973, becoming the seventh and possibly last victim of the Highway 101 Murderer. Her body was discovered near the location of **Cathy Alverson**'s remains. Calan had been bound with white nylon rope and sexually assaulted. Her body had been thrown over the side of a country road into a creek.

▪ **Elaine Calley** was the second confirmed victim of the Highway 101 Murderer. Along with **Mary Spooner**, she was abducted after leaving a Santa Rosa ice skating rink in February 1972. The bodies of the two girls, both 12 years old, were discovered in December 1972. The remains of both victims were found along a steep roadside embankment with their clothes missing. The killer had taken the earrings from each girl. Each had been strangled.

▪ **Samuel Fryman** was a consulting psychologist to the SCCID who first interviewed Byron Avion after his arrest in 1974. He subsequently diagnosed Avion as mentally ill and was instrumental in his eventual institutionalization.

- **Darren Hare** was the District Attorney for Sonoma County at the time of Byron Avion's arrest in 1974.

- **Lynn Howard** was hitchhiking alongside Highway 101 when she vanished without a trace in 1973. The fifteen-year-old became the Highway 101 Murderer's sixth victim. In July of that year, her nude remains were discovered near the location of the bodies of **Mary Spooner** and **Elaine Calley**. Howard had been poisoned with strychnine.

- **Kim Kantell**, like **Cathy Alverson**, was a student at Santa Rosa Junior College. The 20-year-old was last seen hitchhiking near Highway 101 in April 1972. She was presumed to be the fourth victim of the Highway 101 Murderer. In July 1979, the remains of a woman were discovered in a shallow grave at the bottom of a ravine in Sonoma County. Unfortunately, a forensic odontologist was never able to confirm that these remains belonged to Kim Kantell. Consistent with the prior murders, the victim had been bound and strangled with white nylon rope.

- **Samuel Lionell**, San Francisco Police Department (SFPD) homicide investigator. Lionell headed SFPD inquiries into the Zodiac case from 1969 until 1978. In the early years of that investigation, Lionell believed that Byron Avion might have been the fugitive serial killer, Zodiac.

- **Michael ("Mick") Millian**, Detective Sergeant at the SCCID, had been partnered with Manny Bruin in the late 1960s and was later promoted to Sergeant. From early in the case of the Highway 101 Murders, Millian believed that Byron Avion was the killer who had claimed the lives of at least seven girls and women in the Santa Rosa area.

- **Ellen Richard** was the psychologist employed by Berta Baily in Byron Avion's defense effort in 1974. She was convinced that Avion suffered from Multiple Personality Disorder and was therefore probably incapable of committing a seriously violent crime. Her findings were disputed by the consulting psychologist for the SCCID, Samuel Fryman.

- **Mary Spooner** was the first confirmed victim of the Highway 101 Murderer. Along with **Elaine Calley**, she was abducted after leaving a Santa Rosa ice skating rink in February 1972. The bodies of the two girls, both 12 years old, were discovered in December 1972. The remains of both victims were found along a steep roadside embankment with their clothes missing. The killer had taken the earrings from each girl. Each had been strangled.

- **Victor Stinesky, Ph.D.,** Professor of Anthropology at San Francisco University. Stinesky was called into the Highway 101 Murder investigation by Cynthia Turgell, the Sonoma County Medical Examiner. Stinesky was able to positively identify the remains of Mary Spooner and Elaine Calley when they were discovered in 1972. However, he was unable to identify the remains of a teenage female discovered in 1979, presumed to be one of the Highway 101 Murderer's victims.

- **Cynthia Turgell**, Sonoma County Medical Examiner from 1972 until 1997, was intimately involved in the Highway 101 Murder investigation and performed autopsies on several of the victims.

- **Howard Vorhies**, Sonoma County Coroner and (later) Medical Examiner from 1951 until 1972. His position was filled by Cynthia Turgell, the first woman in the history of Sonoma County to hold that post.

Appendix II — An Abbreviated Timeline

Here is an abbreviated timeline of key events that surrounded the Highway 101 Murders and the subsequent investigation:

<u>April 1965</u>: Manny Bruin joins the Sonoma County Sheriff's Office after completing his post-graduate studies at the University of California, Berkeley, in criminal justice. Eighteen months later, he is promoted and assigned to the Sonoma County Criminal Investigations Division (SCCID) as a homicide investigator.

<u>June 1967</u>: Mick Millian, who had worked for three years with the Sonoma County Sheriff's Office, joins the SCCID. He will become Bruin's partner and eventually be promoted to Sergeant, working directly for Bruin in the homicide investigations division.

<u>December 1968</u>: Two teenagers, Betty Lou Jensen and David Faraday, are shot to death in their car in a lover's lane area of Vallejo, east of San Francisco. There are no suspects in the case for six months. Zodiac later claims credit for the double homicide.

<u>July 1969</u>: Zodiac attacks another couple in Vallejo, murdering the woman and seriously injuring her male companion.

<u>September 1969</u>: Zodiac assaults a couple at Lake Berryessa in Napa County, east of Sonoma County. The woman is murdered; her male companion is seriously injured.

<u>Fall 1969</u>: After Zodiac attacks Cecilia Shepherd and Bryan Hartnell on September 27, 1969, at Lake Berryessa, Manny Bruin becomes involved in the investigation, which is sweeping across all San Francisco Bay Area police jurisdictions. During the

ongoing manhunt, more than 2500 suspects are considered, with dozens who reside in Sonoma County. Among the primary suspects at the time is Byron Avion.

October 1969: Zodiac shoots a San Francisco taxicab driver, Paul Stine, in the back of the head, killing him instantly. He then begins a letter-writing campaign to the San Francisco *Chronicle*, which will go on sporadically for years.

Spring 1971: Suspicious that he may be the fugitive Zodiac serial killer, one of Byron Avion's relatives reports her concerns about his strange behavior to SFPD homicide investigators. This event brings Manny Bruin into the Zodiac investigation when SFPD personnel apply for a search warrant on Avion's Santa Rosa apartment.

March 1971: Zodiac writes his last letter to the San Francisco *Chronicle* for nearly three years.

June 1971: Byron Avion's Santa Rosa apartment is searched by SFPD and SCCID investigators. At the time, he is considered to be a viable suspect in the Zodiac case.

Fall 1971: Avion moves permanently from San Francisco to Santa Rosa, to reside with his mother, Jacqueline Avion.

February 1972: Mary Spooner and Elaine Calley are abducted and killed, becoming the first and second victims of the Highway 101 Murderer.

March 1972: Cathy Alverson is abducted and murdered.

April 1972: Cathy Alverson's remains are discovered. Kim Kantell is abducted and murdered.

November 1972: Leslie Buono is abducted and murdered. Howard Vorhies, Medical Examiner for Sonoma County, retires after more than twenty years on the job. His successor is Cynthia Turgell, who becomes intimately involved in the Highway 101 Murder investigation.

December 1972: Leslie Buono's body is discovered. The bodies of Mary Spooner and Elaine Calley are also discovered.

February 1973: Lynn Howard is abducted and murdered.

July 1973: The remains of Lynn Howard are discovered.

December 1973: Terry Calan is abducted and murdered.

January 1974: Zodiac writes to the San Francisco *Chronicle* (the "Exorcist Letter"). The remains of Terry Calan are discovered near the location where Cathy Alverson's body was found in April 1972.

June 1974: Zodiac writes to the San Francisco *Chronicle* (the "Badlands Letter").

Late Summer 1974: Byron Avion is arrested on a variety of charges, including assault and sex crimes against minors. He ultimately pleads "no contest" to the charges and is voluntarily institutionalized on psychiatric grounds. Subsequent to Avion's arrest, the murders in the Santa Rosa area cease.

April 1975: Manny Bruin is promoted to Sergeant at the SCCID.

April 1978: Zodiac writes his last letter to the San Francisco *Chronicle*. Many officers who were close to the investigation later concluded that this letter was a forgery. Its authenticity has never been conclusively proven.

May 1978: Mick Millian is promoted to Sergeant at the SCCID.

July 1979: The remains of a murdered woman are discovered on the outskirts of Santa Rosa. At first, they are thought to be those of Kim Kantell, but a positive identification is never made.

December 1979: Avion is released after five years of institutionalization. Medical personnel at his facility claim that they are certain he does not pose a threat to society.

Winter 1980: Avion is working as a stockman in a large retail store in Santa Rosa. While there, he is accused by a co-worker of harassing a teenage female employee and possibly threatening her life. The alleged victim refuses to file a formal report or to discuss the matter with investigating officers.

Manny Bruin is promoted to Lieutenant at the SCCID. He is later placed in charge of all homicide investigators as a Division Commander.

December 1980: Avion is found dead in the home that he shared with his mother in Santa Rosa. An autopsy and medical investigation indicate a massive heart attack as the probable cause.

May 1981: Byron Avion's mother, Jacqueline, dies of a cerebral hemorrhage in her Santa Rosa home. She leaves no surviving heirs and no one claims her body.

June 1997: Mick Millian retires from the SCCID on his 30th anniversary of law enforcement service.

About the Author:

Michael D. Kelleher is the internationally acclaimed author-scholar of *Profiling the Lethal Employee, Murder Most Rare: the Female Serial Killer* and *When Good Kids Kill*. His writing is truly exemplary, as is reflected by his long list of publishing credits for such venerable houses as Random House, Dell, the Greenwood Publishing Group, and Dead End Street®. Kelleher's work has appeared in the many of the country's major dailies, including the *Washington Post*, the *New York Times* and the San Francisco *Examiner*. He's a frequent guest on both radio and television, including a variety of national news programs.

Also by Michael D. Kelleher:

These are terrible times for Lieutenant Chris Spell, once acclaimed as San Francisco's premiere homicide investigator. At the heart of his beat, the City's chaotic Mission District, women are being systematically murdered, their bodies mutilated and dumped on neighborhood doorsteps. Spell is unable to stop the carnage.

Understaffed, desperate, and beleaguered by the press, the Lieutenant quickly assembles a rag-tag task force to take on the investigation. He recruits the station's forensic psychologist, borrows an old friend and fellow investigator from a neighboring District, and convinces a young, inexperienced beat-cop to join his team. But the killings continue.

Cryptic threats are issued to the press and to Spell's task force. Then, in a stunning act of mayhem, the killer kidnaps the youngest member of the team, a woman with an uncanny resemblance to the half dozen victims he's already claimed.

Out of options and out of time, Spell formulates a plan to get her back and bring the killer down, but the plan might require the life of a second team member. Worse, Spell's prey has already made a last, shocking plan of his own - one his pursuers hadn't considered.

In a final confrontation, orchestrated by the serial killer himself, Spell's world collapses when he learns the killer's motivation and realizes the answers were within his grasp from the very beginning.

Available everywhere fine books are sold.

Dead End Street® highly recommends these titles:

Suzanne Rosewell is the youngest female partner in the history of her prestigious Wall Street law firm. She's a strong, driven woman with  the will to succeed. Then she meets Elias Garner, an enigmatic black Jazz musician who carries an ancient golden trumpet and represents the even more furtive "Chairman" (whom we learn heads the most powerful corporation on earth).

Elias explains that God has always placed among us thirty-six righteous people – each of whom "knows the divine will" and all of which must be accounted for if humanity is to redeem itself. Five are missing from the Chairman's list and Suzanne is asked to set aside her career to search for them. If she is unsuccessful, it appears that the world cannot exist beyond the sunrise.

A painful break-up/breakdown chases 39-year-old Sandy Lowitry from her Silicon Valley home to the Oregon coast in search of answers. Instead, she finds Frosted Glass Man, a fellow tech refugee who left behind a computer-programming job to spend his days harvesting sea glass along Knickerbocker Beach. The strange man's enchanting stories wrap her in a blanket of comfort and wonder, but the whispers of ambition persist and quietly chastise her for settling.

Available everywhere fine books are sold.

ANOTHER FINE OFFERING FROM

DEAD END STREET®

Printed in the United States
40500LVS00003B/37

9 781929 429875